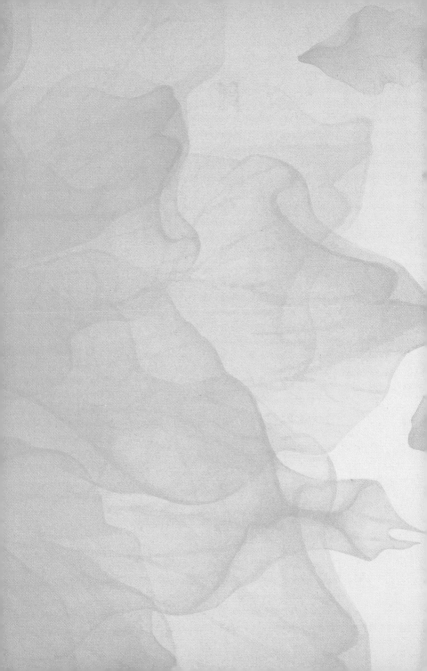

# Live Original

## devotional

### Sadie Robertson

**H**

**HOWARD BOOKS**

An Imprint of Simon & Schuster, Inc.

New York    Nashville    London    Toronto    Sydney    New Delhi

Howard Books
An Imprint of Simon & Schuster, Inc.
1230 Avenue of the Americas
New York, NY 10020

First Howard Books hardcover edition October 2016

HOWARD and colophon are trademarks of Simon & Schuster, Inc.

For information about special discounts for bulk purchases,
please contact Simon & Schuster Special Sales at 1-866-506-1949
or business@simonandschuster.com.

The Simon & Schuster Speakers Bureau can bring authors to your
live event. For more information or to book an event, contact the
Simon & Schuster Speakers Bureau at 1-866-248-3049 or visit our
website at www.simonspeakers.com.

Interior design by Davina Mock-Maniscalco

Manufactured in the United States of America

10   9   8   7   6   5   4   3   2   1

Library of Congress Cataloging-in-Publication Data

Names: Robertson, Sadie, 1997– author.
Title: Live original devotional / Sadie Robertson.
Description: New York : Howard Books, a division of Simon & Schuster, Inc., [2016] |
    Audience: Age 11–14. | Audience: Grade 7 to 8.
Identifiers: LCCN 2016013604| ISBN 9781501126512 (hardcover) |
    ISBN 9781501126529 (ebook)
Subjects: LCSH: Teenage girls—Prayers and devotions—Juvenile literature.
    Christian teenagers—Prayers and devotions—Juvenile literature.
Classification: LCC BV4860 .R63 2016 | DDC 242/.633—dc23
LC record available at https://lccn.loc.gov/2016013604

ISBN 978-1-5011-2651-2
ISBN 978-1-5011-2652-9 (ebook)

# Contents

Hey everyone!

I want to say thank you for all the support you have given me since the beginning of *Duck Dynasty*, through *Dancing with the Stars*, and now on my Live Original Tour. It's been an honor to meet many of you in person and to hear from many of you on social media. Your love and support have meant the world to me and I feel your prayers as I strive to live originally in a world that tries to make us all the same.

I value my quiet time with God and know that you do too. That's the reason I wrote this book. It's a book of fifty-two devotional messages designed to help you in your walk with the Lord. You can use the messages any way you want to use them. You might want to pour over one a week for a year or you might want to work your way through them in fifty-two days. It's totally up to you. The important thing is to spend time every day with God. I have learned that doing this helps me stay strong and well-grounded in the truth.

As young women, the world will constantly throw things at us that are not the truth. The world isn't about telling the truth. It's about making money or gaining power or looking a certain way. But God's word is the truth and, as the scripture tells us, the truth will set you free. Freedom comes from knowing what Jesus has done for you and living a life that reflects that knowledge.

So, I hope you enjoy the messages, but mostly, I pray they inspire you to grow closer to God, love and serve others, and live your own original, God-designed life.

Love, Sadie

Live Original
devotional

## Attitude Check

N O ONE IS CRAZY about sweating. It can make us uncomfortable and smelly. But at times, the best things in life include some parts that aren't so great. Then we have to decide how to respond.

Every summer, I go to one of my very favorite places, Camp Ch-Yo-Ca. I love summers at camp! But when I am there, I know I'm going to sweat!

You might have read about camp in my book *Live Original*, or seen a few pics on Instagram. I go every summer. One of the things we do at camp is called an Attitude Check, which brings me back to sweating. It's hot at camp, and there are bugs and, maybe, a snake or two. In other words, it's not perfect—there are definitely things that make you feel uncomfortable or uneasy. But nothing in life is perfect. That's why one of my grandma's favorite quotes is "If you can't change the situation, change your attitude."

In some ways, camp is like real life. At camp and in real life there are unpleasant parts that you have to either deal with or ignore, but it's worth the effort because, at the same time, there can also be amazing benefits. Some of those benefits for me at camp are learning more about God and His plan for my life and making lifelong friends.

So here's how an Attitude Check works: When the counselors or directors notice the campers dragging around and looking less than excited about being there, one of them will yell, "Attitude Check!" and the campers respond with, "I feel great! Oh, I feel so great!" Then it ends with a loud "Uh!" Seriously, immediately you feel better.

In life, I know you won't feel great every day—there's going to be some sweating—but every day you can find something to feel great about. So the next time you feel down or don't feel like smiling, you might need to challenge yourself to an Attitude Check. Of course, your mom might get a little worried when she hears you yelling out loud about how great you feel, but trust me, when she hears your positive message, she will probably feel great too!

ᕮ ᕤ·°© What Does the Bible Say About It? ©°·ᕤ ᕮ

**Romans 15:5–6 (NIV)**
*May the God who gives endurance and encouragement give you the same attitude of mind toward each other that Christ Jesus had, so that with one mind and one voice you may glorify the God and Father of our Lord Jesus Christ.*

The book of Romans was written with two reasons in mind. First, Paul wanted to be sure the Christians in Rome knew that, because of God's righteousness (or justice), salvation (or deliverance from sin and its consequences) is possible. The best way I can describe God's righteousness is that God is right all the time—and He always does what is right. He is honest and just and worthy and blameless. We cannot be righteous on our own—we can only get righteousness from God.

Read Romans 1:16–17 (NIV) and fill in the blanks.

*For I am not ..................... of the .....................,*
*because it is the power of God that brings ..................... to*
*everyone who believes: first to the .....................,*
*then to the ..................... . For in the gospel the*
*..................... of God is revealed—a righteousness that is*
*by faith from first to last, just as it is written: "The righteous will*
*live by ..................... ."*

And second, Paul wanted to give some instruction on how to live a Christian life.

In Romans 15:5–6, we are told to have the same attitude of mind with each other as who?

..................................................................

..................................................................

If we are to have a good attitude anywhere near that of Jesus, we have to know what His attitude is, and the only way we can do that is by learning more about Him. Keep studying every day to find out who Jesus Christ is and how He lived. Then you will know how to be and to act in a way that honors Him.

## Live It!

Part of living for Jesus is having and presenting the right attitude. Our attitude affects our approach to life. We can choose to approach each day complaining and looking for the bad, or we can approach each day looking for the good. Write our verse for the week, Romans 15:5–6, on a note card and put it up on your bathroom mirror. Say it every morning at least three times. It's a little long, but you can do it. You're looking in the mirror anyway! By the end of the week, this verse will be deep in your heart for you to use whenever you need it.

And go ahead and try that Attitude Check thing. God would love to hear you say, "I feel great! Oh, I feel so great!"

## Ready, Set, Grow!

This week I will strive to keep a good attitude when

. . . . . . . . . . . . . . . . . . . . . . . . . . . . . . . . . . . . . . . . . . .

. . . . . . . . . . . . . . . . . . . . . . . . . . . . . . . . . . . . . . . . . . .

. . . . . . . . . . . . . . . . . . . . . . . . . . . . . . . . . . . . . . . . . . .

# Actions DO Speak Louder Than Words

I'VE GOTTEN TO DO a lot of exciting things. But one of the best and most rewarding has been mission work.

Our church family has what is called a Relief Ministry. Its purpose is just as it sounds—to bring relief to hurting people. I grew up seeing slide shows from around the world of relief work that our church family was involved in. So I was excited when the time came that I could finally go too.

One of my favorite memories is from a mission trip to the Dominican Republic with my mom, grandma (Two-Mama), aunts, and cousins. The trip had its challenges, like the language barrier, but it also had its blessings. It was a great example of how actions speak louder than words.

On this trip my mom, Two-Mama, and I noticed that Maria, one of the little girls in the orphanage, was sleeping on a bed that sank so low in the middle, it nearly touched the ground. I can't even imagine how uncomfortable she must have been sleeping night after night with part of her body basically down in a hole. We knew we had to take action. My mom found a little store that had mattresses, and so she bought her a new mattress, a pillow, and fresh, clean sheets. While I was in the yard playing with Maria, my mom and Two-Mama snuck into her room and set up her new bed. When we brought Maria in to see it, I had never seen such joy. Then the tears came—from all of us! Our sweet little Maria cried tears of joy after seeing what her American family had done for her. We cried tears of thankfulness that God had allowed us to be a part of something so awesome. I learned many lessons that day, but one of them is that even when we can't speak the same language, our actions will do the talking. Actions really DO speak louder than words!

## What Does the Bible Say about It?

**1 John 3:18 (NIV)**
*Dear children, let us not love with words or speech but with actions and in truth.*

## Dig a Little Deeper

This verse isn't giving us permission *not* to use our words for good, but it is a warning that words are not always enough when someone truly needs help.

Have you ever told someone you would do something, but then you didn't?

How did you feel when you didn't follow through with what you promised you would do?

.................................................................

.................................................................

.................................................................

1 John 3:18 tells us we should love with .................
and in ........................ .

Describe a time when your actions showed someone that you love them.

.................................................................

.................................................................

.................................................................

Look at James 1:22. How does this verse compare with 1 John 3:18?

.................................................................

.................................................................

.................................................................

Live It!

This lesson is so important because it gets us thinking of others instead of ourselves. This is a great week to do something for your mom or dad or another family member without being asked to do it. You can clean the kitchen or unload the dishwasher or wash your own clothes. Any of those things would tell your mom or dad that you love them and appreciate them. Or you could volunteer at one of the mission opportunities around your town. I'm sure there are many—all you have to do is ask your friends, your school counselor, your teachers or pastor, or simply search online.

We talked last week about our attitude. Trust me, you will have a hard time not smiling and feeling great if you do something for someone else.

## Ready, Set, Grow!

This week I will show love for others by

........................................................

........................................................

........................................................

........................................................

# Be Happy, Be Joyful

"I JUST WANT TO BE HAPPY." That's what many people say when asked what they want out of life.

Have you ever stopped to think what that really means? Does that mean the person wants to smile all the time or have a peaceful feeling inside or what? I have learned this about happiness: It's how you feel when you praise and thank God, no matter what you're going through. It's being content with what you have. It's also a gift that rubs off on others.

I have a friend named Emma who smiles all the time—I'm not kidding, she really does smile all the time. When Emma walks into a room, you can't help but notice her because of her big smile. And if someone makes a comment that's negative, Emma will find a way to make it positive.

While Emma smiles all the time, I know that every day isn't perfect for her. Over the past six years, she has moved many times. She's had to make new friends and get used to new schools and different teachers, but she has decided to praise God anyway. And that's the key to her happiness. It's a decision she makes every day by giving thanks to God and by focusing on the positive. Emma has discovered that true happiness doesn't depend on what is going on around her; it depends on what is going on inside of her.

Here's one of Emma's Instagram posts. In reading her words, you can understand the joy Emma radiates. Here is part of her post:

> My precious Father. I praise You in gratitude for this weekend! I praise You for growing me—giving me strength to seek Your beautiful presence in every timeless moment. I sing to You in joy for the blessing of getting to play for Your glory. I glorify your mighty name for giving me courage and confidence to give all that I have, yet all at once, my beautiful Savior, you humble me as I know that the strength I have is yours and not my own.

I've learned a lot about happiness, thankfulness, and contentment from Emma. I learned that we should stop trying to find happiness and just *be* happy with wherever we are and whatever we have.

## What Does the Bible Say about It?

**Philippians 4:12–13 (NIV)**

*I know what it is to be in need, and I know what it is to have plenty. I have learned the secret of being content in any and every situation, whether well fed or hungry, whether living in plenty or in want. I can do all this through him who gives me strength.*

In Philippians 4:12 Paul says he has learned a secret. It's interesting that he used the word "learned."

What does that say about Paul's spiritual journey?

. . . . . . . . . . . . . . . . . . . . . . . . . . . . . . . . . . . . . . . . . . . . . . . . . . . . .

. . . . . . . . . . . . . . . . . . . . . . . . . . . . . . . . . . . . . . . . . . . . . . . . . . . . .

. . . . . . . . . . . . . . . . . . . . . . . . . . . . . . . . . . . . . . . . . . . . . . . . . . . . .

Do you think it's hard to be content or happy when times are tough?

. . . . . . . . . . . . . . . . . . . . . . . . . . . . . . . . . . . . . . . . . . . . . . . . . . . . .

. . . . . . . . . . . . . . . . . . . . . . . . . . . . . . . . . . . . . . . . . . . . . . . . . . . . .

. . . . . . . . . . . . . . . . . . . . . . . . . . . . . . . . . . . . . . . . . . . . . . . . . . . . .

Can you think of a time when you complained about an uncomfortable situation instead of making the most of it?

. . . . . . . . . . . . . . . . . . . . . . . . . . . . . . . . . . . . . . . . . . . . . . . . . . . . .

. . . . . . . . . . . . . . . . . . . . . . . . . . . . . . . . . . . . . . . . . . . . . . . . . . . . .

. . . . . . . . . . . . . . . . . . . . . . . . . . . . . . . . . . . . . . . . . . . . . . . . . . . . .

If you apply this verse to the times in your life when you are tempted to complain and grumble, would it change how you act?

. . . . . . . . . . . . . . . . . . . . . . . . . . . . . . . . . . . . . . . . . . . . . . . . . . . . .

. . . . . . . . . . . . . . . . . . . . . . . . . . . . . . . . . . . . . . . . . . . . . . . . . . . . .

. . . . . . . . . . . . . . . . . . . . . . . . . . . . . . . . . . . . . . . . . . . . . . . . . . . . .

Who can give you strength to be happy even when the circumstances are not pleasant?

. . . . . . . . . . . . . . . . . . . . . . . . . . . . . . . . . . . . . . . . . . . . . . . . . .

. . . . . . . . . . . . . . . . . . . . . . . . . . . . . . . . . . . . . . . . . . . . . . . . . .

. . . . . . . . . . . . . . . . . . . . . . . . . . . . . . . . . . . . . . . . . . . . . . . . . .

. . . . . . . . . . . . . . . . . . . . . . . . . . . . . . . . . . . . . . . . . . . . . . . . . .

## Live It!

We're all different. God made us that way. You may or may not be a natural smiler. I know people who are just not smilers on the outside, but they're smilers on the inside. I love how Emma smiles on the outside. Her smile is contagious—you can't help but smile yourself when you look at her. She will tell you that she wasn't always like this, but the more in love she became with Jesus, the more determined she was to show it to the world through smiling. But she would never want what people saw on the outside to be different from what was truly on the inside. This lesson isn't about smiling all the time even if terrible things are happening in your life. This is about really trusting God with those terrible things—then the smile becomes real and genuine.

I'm confident there will be times this week when you can put this lesson into practice. You might not be a happy person when your alarm goes off. If you're not used to smiling, especially first thing in the morning, smiling might be challenging. But remember you *can* do all things through Jesus Christ, who will give you strength. Show the world Jesus lives in you by sharing a smile!

I will smile this week even when

. . . . . . . . . . . . . . . . . . . . . . . . . . . . . . . . . . . . . . . . . . . . . . . . .

. . . . . . . . . . . . . . . . . . . . . . . . . . . . . . . . . . . . . . . . . . . . . . . . .

. . . . . . . . . . . . . . . . . . . . . . . . . . . . . . . . . . . . . . . . . . . . . . . . .

. . . . . . . . . . . . . . . . . . . . . . . . . . . . . . . . . . . . . . . . . . . . . . . . .

*Be Careful What You Say*

I HAVE THIRTY-SIX of my family members living on the same street—crazy, I know. And we love it! We don't ever get tired of each other. In fact, we wish we weren't so busy so we could see each other more. It's the best when I drive past my great-grandma's house and get to wave to her as she comes home from work, or when I honk at my uncle as he pulls up into the driveway on his motorcycle, or when all my cousins come over and we decide to put baby oil on the trampoline and slide around on a rainy day. Many people want to know how we do it: "How do you live so close to each other and still get along?" I've been asked that question over and over.

There really is no secret formula, but there is one thing my great-grandma has always told us that we try hard to put into practice. Mamaw Jo says that *nothing* (and she stresses the word "nothing") is worth hurting the feelings of someone else. That means we are careful to use words that build each other up instead of tearing each other down. That means we keep our mouths closed if we can't think of something nice or pleasant to say. It also means that when there's a choice to include others, we do so. Life in a family as large as ours could be challenging, but it's not because all the adults in our family have shown us how to be careful with our words. They follow my great-grandma's advice and treat each other with kindness.

I'm so blessed to see how people can get along with each other by having it modeled for me. It's how God wants us all to live both within our immediate families and in our church families.

## What Does the Bible Say about It?

**Romans 12:18 (NIV)**
*If it is possible, as far as it depends on you, live at peace with everyone.*

## Dig a Little Deeper

Romans is an important book in the Bible because it tells us what the gospel is and gives us practical advice for how to live a Christ-centered life. When reading Romans 12:18, Paul, the author of Romans, says to live at peace with everyone, but there is a qualification.

What is that?

. . . . . . . . . . . . . . . . . . . . . . . . . . . . . . . . . . . . . . . . . . . . . . . . . . . .

. . . . . . . . . . . . . . . . . . . . . . . . . . . . . . . . . . . . . . . . . . . . . . . . . . . .

. . . . . . . . . . . . . . . . . . . . . . . . . . . . . . . . . . . . . . . . . . . . . . . . . . . .

If you wrote "as far as it depends on me," you got it right. Those words are important because God understands that relationships are difficult and we can't make everyone happy all the time, but we can do our part to help in every situation.

Read Romans 12:16. How does this verse tell us to live with everyone?

. . . . . . . . . . . . . . . . . . . . . . . . . . . . . . . . . . . . . . . . .

. . . . . . . . . . . . . . . . . . . . . . . . . . . . . . . . . . . . . . . . .

. . . . . . . . . . . . . . . . . . . . . . . . . . . . . . . . . . . . . . . . .

In what other situations is harmony important?

. . . . . . . . . . . . . . . . . . . . . . . . . . . . . . . . . . . . . . . . .

. . . . . . . . . . . . . . . . . . . . . . . . . . . . . . . . . . . . . . . . .

. . . . . . . . . . . . . . . . . . . . . . . . . . . . . . . . . . . . . . . . .

How does harmony make a relationship better?

. . . . . . . . . . . . . . . . . . . . . . . . . . . . . . . . . . . . . . . . .

. . . . . . . . . . . . . . . . . . . . . . . . . . . . . . . . . . . . . . . . .

. . . . . . . . . . . . . . . . . . . . . . . . . . . . . . . . . . . . . . . . .

## Live It!

Teenage girls can get a bad reputation for being mean to other girls, so don't get caught in that trap. If you see or hear others talking unkindly to or about others, stand up and let them know it's not right to talk like that. I know it can be uncomfortable to take a stand when others are doing wrong, but God is pretty clear about this. We aren't going to get excused because we're uncomfortable or afraid or because we're teenagers. Nope, it's up to each one of us to show others how people who love God are supposed to act. Come on, girls! Let's show the world that teens can be kind and respectful of each other.

## ❧ Ready, Set, Grow! ❧

This week I will do my best to keep peace when I am

. . . . . . . . . . . . . . . . . . . . . . . . . . . . . . . . . . . . . . . . . . . . . . .

. . . . . . . . . . . . . . . . . . . . . . . . . . . . . . . . . . . . . . . . . . . . . . .

. . . . . . . . . . . . . . . . . . . . . . . . . . . . . . . . . . . . . . . . . . . . . . .

. . . . . . . . . . . . . . . . . . . . . . . . . . . . . . . . . . . . . . . . . . . . . . .

*Climb Your Hill*

THE FALL OF 2014 was a crazy time for me. That was when I was on the TV show *Dancing with the Stars*. I spent thirteen weeks in Los Angeles for the filming of the show. On our first day there, my boyfriend, sister, and Two-Mama (all there to support me) decided we should climb to the top of the hill at Griffith Observatory, where you can get a good look at the famous Hollywood sign.

The weather was perfect, like LA weather always is, so we thought the climb would be easy. Let me just say, it wasn't. That hill was very challenging. Have you ever noticed that getting up is always harder than going down? Yep, anything that involves a climb is going to test your determination to actually make it happen.

About halfway up the hill, I realized that such a difficult climb was going to interfere with what I had come to LA for: to dance. And practice for the TV show was to start the very next day. I needed to be fresh and ready for the job! While I wanted to climb the hill, I soon realized that that climb wasn't the climb I was there for. My climb was going to be *Dancing with the Stars.* Some of the others on the hike wanted to keep climbing, but I knew it wasn't what I should do. I had to be the "bad guy" and stop the trip. It wasn't fun telling everyone that I needed to turn back, but I knew my priorities and my limits—it was what I had to do.

Be careful that you don't get distracted with a hill that isn't yours to climb. Or recognize that maybe it's not the right time to climb a certain hill. We're at the age where many opportunities will come our way. Be prayerful about each of them. Ask God to direct your steps. Even ask your parents or a few trusted friends their opinions. While all "hill climbing" will be challenging, be sure you're climbing a hill that brings glory to God and is in His plan for your life. Then all the effort will be worth it!

## What Does the Bible Say about It?

**Isaiah 48:17 (NIV)**
*This is what the LORD says—your Redeemer, the Holy One of Israel: "I am the LORD your God, who teaches you what is best for you, who directs you in the way you should go."*

## Dig a Little Deeper

Sometimes we don't want to study the Old Testament because it's full of long names we can't pronounce. You might feel that way about reading Isaiah too, but it's a great book that lays out how God had a plan to save the world.

Read the verse above (Isaiah 48:17) and write down the two names for God in the verse.

1. .......................................................................

2. .......................................................................

Now write down the two things in this verse that God does for us.

1. .......................................................................
.......................................................................

2. .......................................................................
.......................................................................

What is something you really want to accomplish in the next few years?

.......................................................................
.......................................................................
.......................................................................

How can what you want to do bring God glory?

.......................................................................
.......................................................................
.......................................................................

Look up Psalm 119:35. What is the result of letting God lead us?

.......................................................................
.......................................................................
.......................................................................

Setting goals is the first step we take to climb the hill of life. Take time to list three goals you have for the next few years. You might have to think on it a little, but no hurry. Whenever you're ready . . .

1. A goal I have for this school year is

. . . . . . . . . . . . . . . . . . . . . . . . . . . . . . . . . . . . . . . . . . . . . . . . . .

. . . . . . . . . . . . . . . . . . . . . . . . . . . . . . . . . . . . . . . . . . . . . . . . . .

. . . . . . . . . . . . . . . . . . . . . . . . . . . . . . . . . . . . . . . . . . . . . . . . . .

2. A more long-term goal I have for my life is

. . . . . . . . . . . . . . . . . . . . . . . . . . . . . . . . . . . . . . . . . . . . . . . . . .

. . . . . . . . . . . . . . . . . . . . . . . . . . . . . . . . . . . . . . . . . . . . . . . . . .

. . . . . . . . . . . . . . . . . . . . . . . . . . . . . . . . . . . . . . . . . . . . . . . . . .

3. A goal I have for telling others about Jesus is

. . . . . . . . . . . . . . . . . . . . . . . . . . . . . . . . . . . . . . . . . . . . . . . . . .

. . . . . . . . . . . . . . . . . . . . . . . . . . . . . . . . . . . . . . . . . . . . . . . . . .

. . . . . . . . . . . . . . . . . . . . . . . . . . . . . . . . . . . . . . . . . . . . . . . . . .

## Ready, Set, Grow!

This week I will determine which hills I need to climb by

. . . . . . . . . . . . . . . . . . . . . . . . . . . . . . . . . . . . . . . . . . . . . . . . . .

. . . . . . . . . . . . . . . . . . . . . . . . . . . . . . . . . . . . . . . . . . . . . . . . . .

. . . . . . . . . . . . . . . . . . . . . . . . . . . . . . . . . . . . . . . . . . . . . . . . . .

## Change Something

I'M SO BLESSED to have an awesome big brother. John Luke continues to challenge me to be the best I can be every day. Don't get me wrong, when we were younger we did our share of pestering each other, but now it's all good and I can say he's one of my best friends.

All through high school, John Luke was constantly challenging himself to change in some way. For a while, he would brush his teeth with his left hand or play Ping-Pong left-handed, even though he is right-handed. I know it sounds like a simple change, but he read somewhere that when we challenge ourselves to make little changes, our brain gets some much-needed exercise. Our hearts and actions need to change too.

For some of us, change is easy. It fits our personality. For others, it's difficult. But for all of us, change will happen whether we choose it or it is chosen for us. So, today, think of an area in your life that you could improve on or where you need a new challenge, and then do what you can to take steps toward that change. Only you decide what gets changed. Don't wait for someone else to make important changes about your life. Maybe you've been hanging around kids who steer you away from Jesus, or you've gotten into the bad habit of hateful thoughts or negative talk. Perhaps you just need to change your morning routine to include some God-time. What is it? Today is the day to take that first step.

## What Does the Bible Say about It?

**James 1:23–24 (NIV)**
*Anyone who listens to the word but does not do what it says is like someone who looks at his face in a mirror and, after looking at himself, goes away and immediately forgets what he looks like.*

## Dig a Little Deeper

I love this verse. I know it doesn't have the word "change" in it, but it's all about change. The book of James is written by Jesus' half brother James. (Can you imagine having Jesus for a brother? No pressure there, right?) The Bible says that James wasn't a follower of Jesus when Jesus was alive and walking the earth (look at John 7:5), but later James came to believe that his brother was God's own Son.

Read 1 Corinthians 15:7 and Galatians 1:19. What caused James to change his mind about Jesus?

When James talked about change, he spoke from personal experience. He knew what it was like to look in the "mirror" of his heart and see what needed to be changed. And when he saw the resurrected Jesus, he changed from being a skeptic to a believer. His book, the book of James, is full of wisdom about how to live a Christian life. He understood that if you truly believe in Jesus Christ as God's Son, and that He died on a cross for your sins, you will experience changes in your life—good changes that will bless you and bring God glory.

Read James 1:23–24 carefully again. Who is James talking to? It's the very first word.

. . . . . . . . . . . . . . . . . . . . . . . . . . . . . . . . . . . . . . . . . . . . . . .

. . . . . . . . . . . . . . . . . . . . . . . . . . . . . . . . . . . . . . . . . . . . . . .

. . . . . . . . . . . . . . . . . . . . . . . . . . . . . . . . . . . . . . . . . . . . . . .

Have you even looked at yourself in the mirror and then turned away and totally forgotten what you saw? No, that never happens. We all look in a mirror to make some change on the outside.

What changes do you typically make when you look in the mirror?

. . . . . . . . . . . . . . . . . . . . . . . . . . . . . . . . . . . . . . . . . . . . . . .

......................................................
......................................................

If your heart could be reflected in a mirror, what would you see? What changes would you want to make?

......................................................
......................................................
......................................................
......................................................
......................................................

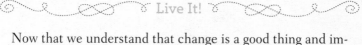

Now that we understand that change is a good thing and important for having a close walk with Jesus, we can start thinking about—and probably feel convicted of—what to change. Change can be difficult or awkward, but it's never impossible with Jesus' help. Try this: Put your hands together—in other words, hold hands with yourself. Now look at your hands and the way the fingers on one hand hold the other hand, and then change them to grip or interlock another way. It's a simple exercise, but a powerful message. We're creatures of habit, so oftentimes change feels funny and awkward at first, but God loves the awkward moments in our lives because that's when we rely more on His strength, and we discover just what we can accomplish when we turn to Him for help. During those times, you'll love seeing how God will turn your changed, and sometimes awkward, moments into something that will *shine*!

❧ Ready, Set, Grow! ❧

This week I will stop . . . . . . . . . . . . . . . . . . . . . . . . . . . . . . . . . and start . . . . . . . . . . . . . . . . . . . . . . . . . . . . .

## Choose Your Fun

M ANY PEOPLE, especially young people, think Christians don't have fun. To those people, I have to say, "You've never hung out with me!" Because I always have fun. Seriously, if you know people who say Christians don't have fun, find out what their definition of "fun" is. I don't define fun as getting drunk or making out with guys at a party. Neither is it riding in a car that's going way over the speed limit or doing something destructive to someone's house. If that's how you define fun, you might consider working on your "fun" definition a little.

The problem for most young people is they let *others* define their fun. A group of kids and some free time can produce some very poor decisions. One person might suggest something crazy to do, and the next thing you know, someone's throwing eggs at cars in parking lots. Okay, maybe that hasn't happened to you, but something similar probably has. Fun activities are just like everything else we do in life: they're a choice. And for that choice to be a good one, it needs to come from someplace more meaningful than "I just want to feel a rush," or "I just want to do what my friends are doing." Our enjoyment should come from a smarter place than that. A smarter place would be a heart that respects others and their property and looks out for their good.

When you want to have a good time, choose activities that are good for everyone so that, once the fun is over, everyone is smiling. One thing I like about John Luke is that he loves to help others have fun, but he never does it at the expense of someone else's feelings or reputation. One time he decided his class at school needed a fun party, so he threw a Jell-O party. To get into the party, you needed to bring a big bowl of green Jell-O. All the Jell-O was dumped into a blow-up swimming pool and then the fun began. I love that John Luke was creative about planning fun activities for his friends to do where everyone had a good time and they could celebrate their hard work together.

## What Does the Bible Say about It?

**Psalm 68:3 (NIV)**
*But may the righteous be glad and rejoice before God; may they be happy and joyful.*

## Dig a Little Deeper

Psalms is a book in the Bible that is made up of songs. The verse above is a small part of a very long song. Since I have been to church my whole life, I've learned to recognize that a lot of worship songs we sing take lyrics from the book of Psalms. You might notice that at your church too. The songs in Psalms don't seem to rhyme like songs do today, but we can still understand their meaning and appreciate their message.

Look at the beginning of Chapter 68. Who is this Psalm for?

........................................................

........................................................

........................................................

Many of the Psalms have directions like this. Psalms were songs of worship just like we sing today. The Psalms tell us different characteristics of God. Read each verse and write the characteristic of God found in that verse.

**Psalm 68:5**
*A father to the fatherless, a defender of widows, is God in his holy dwelling.*

........................................................

........................................................

........................................................

**Psalm 68:19**
*Praise be to the Lord, to God our Savior, who daily bears our burdens.*

........................................................

........................................................

........................................................

**Psalm 68:20**

*Our God is a God who saves; from the Sovereign* LORD *comes escape from death.*

. . . . . . . . . . . . . . . . . . . . . . . . . . . . . . . . . . . . . . . . . . . . . . . . . . . . . . .

. . . . . . . . . . . . . . . . . . . . . . . . . . . . . . . . . . . . . . . . . . . . . . . . . . . . . . .

. . . . . . . . . . . . . . . . . . . . . . . . . . . . . . . . . . . . . . . . . . . . . . . . . . . . . . .

 Live It!

I like to listen to all types of music—you probably do too—so I'm grateful that we have great Christian music to choose from today. I'm also blessed to be friends with many popular recording artists. Do you think the Christian musical artists in Bible days were celebrities? Maybe some were, but probably most were men and women who loved God with all their heart and used music to express their love for Him. I'm happy to say that the Christian recording artists I know are the same way—they love God, and their music is an expression of that love. If you haven't been exposed to Christian music, I want to encourage you to find a Christian radio station and start listening to it every day. In fact, I'd like to challenge you to listen to nothing but Christian music for one full week. When you let God's Word pour into you through a song, your day will be more joyful, your decisions will be more God-focused, your heart will be more in tune with His love for you, and your choices will be more in line with what He would have you do.

## Ready, Set, Grow!

This week I will set my radio on . . . . . . . . . . . . . . . . . . . . . . . . . . . . . . . . . . . .
I will let God speak to me through . . . . . . . . . . . . . . . . . . . . . . . . . . . . . . . .

. . . . . . . . . . . . . . . . . . . . . . . . . . . . . . . . . . . . . . . . . . . . . . . . . . . . . . . . . . . . . . . .

. . . . . . . . . . . . . . . . . . . . . . . . . . . . . . . . . . . . . . . . . . . . . . . . . . . . . . . . . . . . . . . .

. . . . . . . . . . . . . . . . . . . . . . . . . . . . . . . . . . . . . . . . . . . . . . . . . . . . . . . . . . . . . . . .

## Confidence Is Key

HAVE YOU EVER MET SOMEONE who seems to have been born with confidence? My little sister, Bella, is one of those people. When she was just a toddler, she would roll down the back window of the car and yell her order to the attendant at the drive-through window. To this day, this trait is serving her well. She's not afraid to ask anyone for a selfie, including the One Direction guys. (Okay, I know it's not the most important thing in life, but it's fun.) I love how Bella is not ashamed or embarrassed to talk to anyone.

Having confidence is being sure of yourself and sure of what you are about to do. By that, I mean you're confident in who you are as a person because you often have your parents' or friends' encouragement and support.

For many things we do in life, confidence is a game changer. It's that edge that can take a person from being good at something to being great. There are many talented people who don't live up to their potential because they lack confidence. On the other hand, confidence can also be lost after failing at something or if others keep saying you don't measure up. Take Bella, for example. If my mom and others in her life shot down everything she did, her God-given confidence would start to fade.

Did you know that the Bible is full of people who didn't have confidence? It's true. I love that God used men and women who weren't always trained for the job they were asked to do. He did this to show them (and us) that, with His help, we can do far more than we might ever think. Look at Joshua. (Seriously, look at him. Turn to the book of Joshua in your Bible and start reading.) Joshua was given the job of leading the Israelites into the Promised Land after the death of Moses. And just like us, he knew he couldn't do it alone—he needed God's help to pull this job off successfully. Anything you attempt to do in life will go better with God's help and encouragement. So, you really don't need self-confidence; you need God's-confidence living in you.

 What Does the Bible Say about It?

**Joshua 1:9 (NIV)**
*Have I not commanded you? Be strong and courageous. Do not be afraid; do not be discouraged, for the L*ORD *your God will be with you wherever you go.*

Joshua was a nervous leader. After all, he was basically Moses' assistant who was given the job of taking the city of Jericho and leading the Israelites into the Promised Land. At that time, cities were protected by stone walls. Jericho's wall is believed to have been up to twenty-six feet high and sat on top of a forty-six foot wide embankment. No wonder Joshua was nervous. How could he possibly attack such a mighty structure?

Read Joshua 1:6–7 and Joshua 1:9. Three times God told Joshua to be ........................ and ........................ .

Here's the good news. Joshua wasn't given anything that we aren't given as well.

Read Joshua 1:5. What promise does God give Joshua?

........................................................................

........................................................................

........................................................................

........................................................................

Read Joshua 1:7. What is the key to being successful?

........................................................................

........................................................................

........................................................................

........................................................................

Read Joshua 1:9. Who will always be with Joshua?

. . . . . . . . . . . . . . . . . . . . . . . . . . . . . . . . . . . . . . . . . . . . . . . . . .

. . . . . . . . . . . . . . . . . . . . . . . . . . . . . . . . . . . . . . . . . . . . . . . . . .

. . . . . . . . . . . . . . . . . . . . . . . . . . . . . . . . . . . . . . . . . . . . . . . . . .

. . . . . . . . . . . . . . . . . . . . . . . . . . . . . . . . . . . . . . . . . . . . . . . . . .

~ Live It! ~

Knowing something and living something are two different things. Our heads can know something to be true, yet we can still struggle with living like it's true.

Take your Bible and underline or highlight Joshua 1:9. The first few words tell us this is a command. Commands are more than suggestions—they are more like an order, and something we must do. God is making it very clear that we must be strong and courageous to tackle the "Jericho" in our life. It's true you won't face a stone wall, but you will face other big obstacles that might discourage you. But when you are strong and courageous, you will have the confidence you need to face whatever is in front of you.

In what areas of life do you lack confidence and rely on your own strength?

. . . . . . . . . . . . . . . . . . . . . . . . . . . . . . . . . . . . . . . . . . . . . . . . . .

. . . . . . . . . . . . . . . . . . . . . . . . . . . . . . . . . . . . . . . . . . . . . . . . . .

. . . . . . . . . . . . . . . . . . . . . . . . . . . . . . . . . . . . . . . . . . . . . . . . . .

. . . . . . . . . . . . . . . . . . . . . . . . . . . . . . . . . . . . . . . . . . . . . . . . . .

Now write these areas on a separate sheet of paper. Underneath them write these words:

*I will face these areas in my life with strength and courage because God is with me.*

## Ready, Set, Grow!

This week I will boldly face the obstacles in my life by

..................................................................................

..................................................................................

..................................................................................

..................................................................................

## Different Is Good

HAVE YOU EVER FELT DIFFERENT from other kids? I remember the first time I felt different. At thirteen years old I was invited to travel to Austria to play basketball for a Junior Olympic team. Now that I am older, I realize that thirteen is a time when most kids feel different anyway, but up to that time, I thought I was just a normal kid living a normal life. Once I arrived in Austria and met my American roommates, I knew I was very different from them. Besides the fact that they were both northern girls and I'm a very southern girl with different customs, they had not grown up going to church.

This was the first time I realized that people who believe in God act a certain way—a different way than people who don't believe in Him. I had basically spent thirteen years with other Christians just like me. This was my first exposure to boy talk, cusswords, and partying. (Trust me, my eyes were probably locked in a stare!) I had to make some tough decisions on the spot, and if you're a Christian, they're ones you have to make too. I remember calling my mom and telling her how different everyone was. She gave me great advice. She told me to focus on my job there, which was to play basketball, and realize my teammates didn't know what I knew about God.

I guess the question about being different always goes back to this: Who is the different one? Was I the different one, or were my teammates? The answer to that question is: it depends on the situation. If these girls found themselves at the summer Christian camp I go to, they would be the different ones. But they didn't. I was on their territory. I was the different one. The good thing about being different is, because you will stand out, you can have an impact on the others around you. I realized I had a job to do: I had to show these girls what someone who believes in God acts like. I had to use my differentness to make a difference.

I'm happy to say that I still have a relationship with some of the girls I met on that trip. I value the experience so much, and it will forever be one of the most important learning experiences of my life.

## What Does the Bible Say about It?

**Romans 12:2 (NIV)**
*Do not conform to the pattern of this world, but be transformed by the renewing of your mind. Then you will be able to test and approve what God's will is—his good, pleasing and perfect will.*

Read Romans 12:2. What instruction is found in this verse?

. . . . . . . . . . . . . . . . . . . . . . . . . . . . . . . . . . . . . . . . . . . . . . . . .

. . . . . . . . . . . . . . . . . . . . . . . . . . . . . . . . . . . . . . . . . . . . . . . . .

. . . . . . . . . . . . . . . . . . . . . . . . . . . . . . . . . . . . . . . . . . . . . . . . .

Can you think of a pattern you'd use to make something for yourself?

. . . . . . . . . . . . . . . . . . . . . . . . . . . . . . . . . . . . . . . . . . . . . . . . .

. . . . . . . . . . . . . . . . . . . . . . . . . . . . . . . . . . . . . . . . . . . . . . . . .

. . . . . . . . . . . . . . . . . . . . . . . . . . . . . . . . . . . . . . . . . . . . . . . . .

You might have said a pattern to make clothes. My Two-Mama sews, and I have several beautiful little dresses she made for me when I was younger. I used to love watching her lay a pattern on the fabric. She would tell me that a pattern is used so that when the fabric is sewn together, the pieces will fit together exactly right to create a garment. But this verse says for us *not* to conform to, or follow, the pattern of the world. If we do, we'll fit in with the world instead of with God.

Name two things you see that the world says are okay to do but the Bible says are not okay.

1. . . . . . . . . . . . . . . . . . . . . . . . . . . . . . . . . . . . . . . . . . . . . . . .

. . . . . . . . . . . . . . . . . . . . . . . . . . . . . . . . . . . . . . . . . . . . . . . . .

2. . . . . . . . . . . . . . . . . . . . . . . . . . . . . . . . . . . . . . . . . . . . . . . .

. . . . . . . . . . . . . . . . . . . . . . . . . . . . . . . . . . . . . . . . . . . . . . . . .

We are told to renew our minds. What does it mean to renew something?

. . . . . . . . . . . . . . . . . . . . . . . . . . . . . . . . . . . . . . . . . . . . . . . . . . . . . . . . . . . . . . . . . . . . . . . . . . . . . . . . . . . . . .

. . . . . . . . . . . . . . . . . . . . . . . . . . . . . . . . . . . . . . . . . . . . . . . . . . . . . . . . . . . . . . . . . . . . . . . . . . . . . . . . . . . . . .

. . . . . . . . . . . . . . . . . . . . . . . . . . . . . . . . . . . . . . . . . . . . . . . . . . . . . . . . . . . . . . . . . . . . . . . . . . . . . . . . . . . . . .

. . . . . . . . . . . . . . . . . . . . . . . . . . . . . . . . . . . . . . . . . . . . . . . . . . . . . . . . . . . . . . . . . . . . . . . . . . . . . . . . . . . . . .

A driver's license is a good example of something that has to be renewed. That tells the authorities that we are keeping our driving skills up to date. God wants us to constantly renew our minds, keeping our Godly skills up to date. That happens by reading God's Word and talking to Him through prayer. When we do this, it will be easier for us to know what God's will is for our life.

Live It!

I have a challenge for you: when you are faced with a situation where you know you will be different, don't back away from it. But this challenge comes with a warning: be sure to know yourself—know your limits and capabilities. Don't get in a situation where you won't be able to stand up for what is right. The Bible warns us to flee from sinful situations. That means to run. Being able to stand strong in our teen years can be hard because there's so much pressure to fit in. If you know you are not the person who can resist certain temptations, don't put yourself in the middle of them. Approach those situations cautiously and consider getting a friend who is strong in those areas to help you.

You can start with small things, like speaking up in your group of friends when someone uses bad language or by refusing to listen to gossip. Just say you're not interested in hearing about that subject or even change the subject altogether. Soon your friends will know that bad language and gossip are not things you are going to tolerate. Always remember your "different" behavior has to be wrapped in love and kindness. No one wants to be told or shown something by someone who acts like a sassy pants, as my little sister sometimes calls our brothers. This would be a great week to practice your "I am different" skills.

### ❧ Ready, Set, Grow! ❧

This week I will show someone I am different by

........................................................................

........................................................................

........................................................................

........................................................................

## Disappointments Happen

'VE ALWAYS BEEN ATHLETIC and have played nearly every sport. When I was in middle school, I tried out for cheerleading and made the team. But after cheering for one year, I came to the conclusion that cheering wasn't for me and decided to concentrate on other sports. As I was finishing up my freshman year of high school, my cheerleading friends talked me into trying out again for the upcoming school year. Well, I tried out, but I didn't make the team. While I was happy for my friends who made the team, I have to admit, I was disappointed. I felt like I would be missing out on the fun things they would be doing, and I was embarrassed that I didn't have the skills to make the team. Disappointments come when our expectations are not realized. No matter how hard we try to brace ourselves, handling disappointments can be tricky.

I know that I will have more serious disappointments than not making the cheer team. I also know that by learning to handle the smaller disappointments, I am preparing for the harder ones. The disappointment of not making the cheer team showed me several things:

1. Everyone has their own set of disappointments to think about. They're not necessarily paying attention to my disappointment.

2. Life will go on.

3. Fun things await even noncheerleaders.

What I'm trying to say is, disappointments are a part of life. No one will escape them. When one comes your way, look at it for what it is: a time to learn and grow.

## What Does the Bible Say about It?

**Jeremiah 29:11–13 (NIV)**

*"For I know the plans I have for you," declares the Lord, "plans to prosper you and not to harm you, plans to give you hope and a future. Then you will call on me and come and pray to me, and I will listen to you. You will seek me and find me when you seek me with all your heart."*

## Dig a Little Deeper

Most of our disappointments are the result of not getting what we want, like being a cheerleader or getting a certain job. Jeremiah 29:11–15 shows that God cares about you and he cares about your dreams and goals. But we have to trust that God knows what is best for us. Many times what we think is best isn't what God *knows* is best. Think about a roller coaster ride. Most of us ride them and love them, but seriously, it's a crazy ride, so why do we do it? One reason is that we have seen the end of the ride, where everyone gets off laughing. God knows the end of our ride—He knows our whole life story. We haven't seen the end of the roller coaster, but He has. But it's one thing to be disappointed with our life, and it's a much bigger thing to be a disappointment to God.

Let's look at Jeremiah. He was a young prophet of God with a mission to tell the people of his day that they were disappointing God. Jeremiah warned Israel that God was not happy with their choices and they needed to repent of their evil ways. God was warning His people, through Jeremiah, that the rest of their story would not be good if they continued in the path they were walking. But if they would repent and follow God, they would have a happy ending.

Have you ever felt like your life was a roller coaster?

...............................................................

...............................................................

...............................................................

...............................................................

What ups and downs have you experienced lately?

...............................................................

...............................................................

...............................................................

...............................................................

What keeps you from trusting God and turning all of your life over to Him?

. . . . . . . . . . . . . . . . . . . . . . . . . . . . . . . . . . . . . . . . . . . . . . . . . . . . . . . . . . .

. . . . . . . . . . . . . . . . . . . . . . . . . . . . . . . . . . . . . . . . . . . . . . . . . . . . . . . . . . .

. . . . . . . . . . . . . . . . . . . . . . . . . . . . . . . . . . . . . . . . . . . . . . . . . . . . . . . . . . .

. . . . . . . . . . . . . . . . . . . . . . . . . . . . . . . . . . . . . . . . . . . . . . . . . . . . . . . . . . .

Have you ever trusted someone who let you down?

. . . . . . . . . . . . . . . . . . . . . . . . . . . . . . . . . . . . . . . . . . . . . . . . . . . . . . . . . . .

. . . . . . . . . . . . . . . . . . . . . . . . . . . . . . . . . . . . . . . . . . . . . . . . . . . . . . . . . . .

. . . . . . . . . . . . . . . . . . . . . . . . . . . . . . . . . . . . . . . . . . . . . . . . . . . . . . . . . . .

God will never let you down. You can trust that He has your back in all things. This is not to say you won't have disappointments—you will. But if you truly trust that God is with you, you will look at those disappointments as "appointments" with God to do something mighty in your life.

## Live It!

Fill in the blanks in this statement according to Jeremiah 29:11–13.

*I know God has* . . . . . . . . . . . . . *to* . . . . . . . . . . . . . . . . . . . . . *me and not to* . . . . . . . . . . . . . . . . . . . *me. He has plans to give me* . . . . . . . . . . . *and a* . . . . . . . . . . . *. I will* . . . . . . . . . . . *to Him and* . . . . . . . . . . . *to Him, and He will listen. I will* . . . . . . . . . . . *Him and* . . . . . . . . . . . . . . . . . . . *Him.*

Living like we really believe this statement will change how we view the disappointments in our life. It will be easier to say, "God, you know what is best for me. I trust you."

## Ready, Set, Grow!

The next time I feel disappointed about something I will

. . . . . . . . . . . . . . . . . . . . . . . . . . . . . . . . . . . . . . . . . . . . . . . . . . . . . . . . .

. . . . . . . . . . . . . . . . . . . . . . . . . . . . . . . . . . . . . . . . . . . . . . . . . . . . . . . . .

. . . . . . . . . . . . . . . . . . . . . . . . . . . . . . . . . . . . . . . . . . . . . . . . . . . . . . . . .

. . . . . . . . . . . . . . . . . . . . . . . . . . . . . . . . . . . . . . . . . . . . . . . . . . . . . . . . .

*Discover Your Gifts*

THERE IS SO MUCH TALENT constantly displayed over social media. With YouTube, Instagram, Snapchat, Periscope, and Facebook, you can constantly see friends and strangers who can sing, dance, play guitar, do a magic trick, turn a cartwheel, or eat a hundred hot dogs in five minutes.

Seeing so much talent can be intimidating. If you're like me, you've had a moment or two where you've thought, "Wow! I wish I could do that!" Tempting us to compare ourselves to others is one of Satan's best tricks to make us feel like we don't measure up. If Satan can convince you or me that we are not gifted in any way, he can keep us from God's plans for our life.

Here's the deal—thinking you don't have any gifts is believing in a lie. You might not be able to sing, dance, or eat a lot of hot dogs, but you do have a talent—everyone does. Remember this: most of the talents we see on social media are not the ones God loves to see us perform. If God made social media posts, they would look like this: Josh just made a sick child laugh, or Savannah is baking cookies for her elderly neighbor, or Jeremy is sharing the hope of Jesus with a homeless person. While God gifts His children with the ability to sing or dance, He also gifts us with the ability to serve others. It's a talent we all have and one He loves to see us use.

**James 1:17 (NIV)**
*Every good and perfect gift is from above, coming down from the Father of the heavenly lights, who does not change like shifting shadows.*

## Dig a Little Deeper

When we think of talents or gifts, we think of things like singing or playing the piano. But the Bible lists other things as gifts, and when we understand how important they are to the kingdom of God, we will learn to value what God values. The verse above tells us that every good gift comes from God. Look at Romans 12:6–8. List seven gifts God values.

1. .............................................................
   .............................................................
2. .............................................................
   .............................................................
3. .............................................................
   .............................................................
4. .............................................................

5. ........................................................

........................................................

6. ........................................................

........................................................

7. ........................................................

........................................................

## Live It!

Finding our talent can be tricky. Many people sit around waiting for their "gift" to reveal itself. Don't do that! Just start serving and your gift will rise to the top. Try a lot of things—teach a class or organize an event. Try playing an instrument or visiting the sick or singing on the worship team. You will never know what you're good at until you get out there and try. If you discover something is not for you, just move on to something else. When one thing doesn't work out, that doesn't mean you failed. It means you tried, and God is always happy with that.

## Ready, Set, Grow!

Today I will seek to discover my gifts by

........................................................

........................................................

........................................................

........................................................

*Dream Big*

I HAVE ALWAYS BEEN A DREAMER. Sometimes that's not a good thing because I tend to daydream when I should be doing homework or reading a book. But, mostly, dreaming is great. I'm surrounded by dreamers. From great-grandparents down to cousins, my family has the "dream gene," as I called it in my book *Live Original*.

Our first experiences with dreams are when we are very young and we wake up and tell our mom some crazy story that happened when we were asleep. Then Mom will say, "You must have had a dream." But as we get older, we begin to daydream. Daydreams are imaginary too, but not in a crazy, random way—they are things we hope and plan for that could actually come true. I think Walt Disney got it right in the song from *Cinderella* that says a dream is a wish your heart makes. Don't you love that? Even better than Walt Disney, God says in Psalm 37:4 (NIV), "Take delight in the LORD, and he will give you the desires of your heart." The desires of our heart are the things we dream about.

In order for a dream to have a chance of coming true, we

have to first imagine it. That means we have to use some brainpower and quiet time to set our thoughts free to think through possibilities for our life, no matter how crazy they may seem at the time.

In today's world it's hard to be alone and be still and quiet. There are so many distractions. We've always got a friend to text, Snapchat, Instagram, or Periscope away. But dreaming requires you to carve out some time to be alone and use the brain God gave you to think and dream and pray and maybe even plan.

So don't be afraid to dream big. And remember, God is way bigger than Walt Disney. God knows what is needed and has the ability to help make your dreams come true.

## What Does the Bible Say about It?

**1 John 5:14–15 (NIV)**
*This is the confidence we have in approaching God: that if we ask anything according to his will, he hears us. And if we know that he hears us—whatever we ask—we know that we have what we asked of him.*

## Dig a Little Deeper

What have you asked for lately that your parents got for you?

. . . . . . . . . . . . . . . . . . . . . . . . . . . . . . . . . . . . . . . . . . . . .

. . . . . . . . . . . . . . . . . . . . . . . . . . . . . . . . . . . . . . . . . . . . .

Circle your answer:

When I ask my parents for something, I am usually *confident / not confident* that they will get it for me.

Read 1 John 5:14–15 closely and fill in the blanks.

*If we ask . . . . . . . . . . . . . . . . . according to His . . . . . . . . . . . . . . . . . , He will hear us.*

Sometimes we ask our parents for things that would not be good for us to have.

Do you think we do that with God too?

. . . . . . . . . . . . . . . . . . . . . . . . . . . . . . . . . . . . . . . . . . . . . . . . . . . . . . .

. . . . . . . . . . . . . . . . . . . . . . . . . . . . . . . . . . . . . . . . . . . . . . . . . . . . . . .

. . . . . . . . . . . . . . . . . . . . . . . . . . . . . . . . . . . . . . . . . . . . . . . . . . . . . . .

The scripture tells us our requests need to be "according to His will."

Look up Proverbs 3:5–6. We're told to trust in the Lord and lean not on . . . . . . . . . . . . . . . . . . . . . . . . understanding. When we pray about and seek to know God's dreams for us, and we trust Him with those dreams, we can be ready for a dream-come-true kind of life.

Have you ever gone to bed at night and wished to dream a certain dream? It's hard to make that happen, isn't it? Most likely we dream about some pretty crazy things that we don't want to dream about, like forgetting our locker combination at school or going to school in our pajamas. We don't have much control over our dreams at night, but we *can* control our hopes and dreams for our future.

I like to make something I call a dream jar. Take a jar of any size and a stack of magazines. Look through the magazines and cut out any pictures or words that convey your hopes and dreams for the future. Once you have a pretty good stack, just glue them right on the jar. After they are on the jar, cover the entire jar with a sealer like Mod Podge. Once it dries, you will have a great reminder of the dreams you have for your life. The fun part will come in twenty-five years or more when you take it out and see how many of your dreams came true.

## Ready, Set, Grow!

This week I will trust God with my dreams by

. . . . . . . . . . . . . . . . . . . . . . . . . . . . . . . . . . . . . . . . . . . . . .

. . . . . . . . . . . . . . . . . . . . . . . . . . . . . . . . . . . . . . . . . . . . . .

. . . . . . . . . . . . . . . . . . . . . . . . . . . . . . . . . . . . . . . . . . . . . .

. . . . . . . . . . . . . . . . . . . . . . . . . . . . . . . . . . . . . . . . . . . . . .

*Energizers from God*

WHAT DO YOU DO to get extra energy? My mom drinks a Coke. My Mamaw Kay has a Coke Zero. My great-grandma reaches for the coffee—black (that means no cream or sugar—ugh!). Apparently, we have become a nation in need of more energy, which might explain why we see such long lines at every Starbucks. I admit, I am one of their faithful customers. I can taste it now—a Hazelnut Frappuccino. Yum! Well, coffee is one way to get extra energy, but there are other ways too.

At summer camp, we do what we call "energizers." Energizers are short dances to fast music intended get us up and moving. Since most kids love music and love to dance, energizers are as successful as a Frappuccino. One song and we're all on our feet, full of energy.

One day I was thinking about that word "energizers," so I looked up some synonyms. Here they are: "pick-me-ups," "refreshers," "boosts," "liveners." Then it hit me: God is so awesome because He always goes the extra mile to give me what I need. The Bible tells us that every good and perfect thing comes from God. That means even a mocha (another fav).

This may be a time when you're suffering from heartache and pain. But know this: God loves you and He wants to refresh you. He wants to give you a pick-me-up.

Even better than a latte is an open Bible. I have found that nothing picks me up better than God speaking to me through His Word. So, next time you need to feel refreshed, go ahead, get your latte, but also read a sweet message from your heavenly Father. His Word is the ultimate energizer!

## What Does the Bible Say about It?

**Isaiah 40:31 (NIV)**
*Those who hope in the LORD will renew their strength. They will soar on wings like eagles; they will run and not grow weary, they will walk and not be faint.*

## Dig a Little Deeper

I love that the Bible is written with word-pictures. Since my brain goes faster than it should most of the time, I need word-pictures to help me slow down and understand what I'm reading.

In Isaiah 40:31, we're told that when we put our hope in the Lord, He will renew our strength and we will . . . . . . . . . . . . on wings like eagles. My school mascot is an eagle, so I have heard this verse all through my school years. It has always inspired me.

I love that word "soar." Don't you? Other words for "soar" are "aspire," "sail," and "skyrocket." That's a good one—"skyrocket"! How great is it to know that God will skyrocket us to greatness when we put our hope in Him.

Keep reading this verse and fill in the blanks: We will run and ..................... and walk and ........................ .

## Live It!

Life is full of situations that can cause us to be sad or drain us of energy. Today, you may be extra tired from staying up too late studying, or maybe you played a basketball or volleyball game last night and you're sore. Sometimes we can genuinely be tired! But sometimes what seems like a tired feeling might really be sadness or worry. Life itself can drain us of energy. Things like dealing with classmates who are cruel or handling grown-up situations because of a home life in crisis can exhaust us.

Whenever you are going through a time that leaves you feeling tired and worn out, there are a few things you can do. Number one is open your Bible and read. We're told that God's Word is powerful and capable of changing hearts. Just reading God's Word can give your energy. Number two, pray for God to give you the strength and energy you need. Remember we've already learned that God will give you the desires of your heart, so trust Him at His Word. Number three (this may just work for me, but try it), do something physical, like take a walk and notice God's creation or Hula-Hoop or jump rope. Do something that's gets your body going.

### ✿ Ready, Set, Grow! ✿

This week I will come to trust God as my energizer by

. . . . . . . . . . . . . . . . . . . . . . . . . . . . . . . . . . . . . . . . . . . . . . . . . . . . .

. . . . . . . . . . . . . . . . . . . . . . . . . . . . . . . . . . . . . . . . . . . . . . . . . . . . .

. . . . . . . . . . . . . . . . . . . . . . . . . . . . . . . . . . . . . . . . . . . . . . . . . . . . .

. . . . . . . . . . . . . . . . . . . . . . . . . . . . . . . . . . . . . . . . . . . . . . . . . . . . .

## Fame Is Fleeting

I WAS FOURTEEN when our TV show *Duck Dynasty* started. Like most things in life, on one hand it seems like the show started yesterday, but on the other hand it seems like we've done it *forever*. Since the beginning of the show, I have heard the phrase "Fame is fleeting." This was usually said along with these words: "Don't get too used to it."

I don't know who originally said "Fame is fleeting," but I have figured out it's true, at least partly. That statement simply means that being famous or doing something great doesn't mean the notoriety you get will last. I think of my two awesome great-grandfathers. Each of them served our country during wartime, founded ministries that are still functioning today, and were involved in changing their communities for the better. They were well-known and well-respected. In fact, both of them have a building, plaque, or some other such thing named for them. I think it's great to see that some of the things they worked so hard to accomplish are still being used or recognized today.

However, it probably won't be many more years that either

of my great-grandfathers' names will still be recognized outside of our family. In this way, fame is fleeting. If you follow sports at all, you see this every season. The sports team that is on top and in all the headlines for a few years eventually drops to the bottom with very little said about them. That's life. Fame is fleeting.

I'm grateful for the time our family has had to make an impact on the world, and I don't want to take the opportunities we've had lightly. But I'm not scared by the "fame is fleeting" comments. I know my fame is fleeting, but I also know God's fame—His mark, His presence throughout eternity—is not. Anything I can do to bring attention and glory to His name will have forever consequences. I don't want to get caught up in the lie that says everything dies away anyway, so why should we bother? God is very clear that our time here on earth is to be spent working and doing things that bring Him glory and make the world a better place for everyone. My great-grandfathers' times on earth are over. Their days of accomplishing great things have long passed. But because of their love for God and our family, a part of them lives on through me, my siblings, and my cousins.

I guess a certain kind of fame is fleeting, but for us believers, God-given fame is forever.

**Matthew 6:20 (NIV)**

*But store up for yourselves treasures in heaven, where moths and vermin do not destroy, and where thieves do not break in and steal.*

———— Dig a Little Deeper ————

Psalm 39 was written by King David. Remember, the Psalms are songs. This is a really sad song, maybe even written for a funeral. As David pours out his sorrows to God, he asks Him to show him or remind him that life is short.

Read Psalm 39:4. Why do you think David wants to be reminded of how fleeting his life on earth is?

......................................................
......................................................
......................................................

If you could know how many days you had to live on earth, would it change how you live?

......................................................
......................................................
......................................................

List some things you would do if you only had one year to live.

1. ....................................................
......................................................

2. . . . . . . . . . . . . . . . . . . . . . . . . . . . . . . . . . . . . . . . . . . . . . . .

. . . . . . . . . . . . . . . . . . . . . . . . . . . . . . . . . . . . . . . . . . . . . . . .

3. . . . . . . . . . . . . . . . . . . . . . . . . . . . . . . . . . . . . . . . . . . . . . . .

. . . . . . . . . . . . . . . . . . . . . . . . . . . . . . . . . . . . . . . . . . . . . . . .

Since we know our time on earth is short, what does Matthew 6:20 tell us about storing our treasure?

. . . . . . . . . . . . . . . . . . . . . . . . . . . . . . . . . . . . . . . . . . . . . . . .

. . . . . . . . . . . . . . . . . . . . . . . . . . . . . . . . . . . . . . . . . . . . . . . .

. . . . . . . . . . . . . . . . . . . . . . . . . . . . . . . . . . . . . . . . . . . . . . . .

. . . . . . . . . . . . . . . . . . . . . . . . . . . . . . . . . . . . . . . . . . . . . . . .

 Live It! 

No matter if you live 15 years or 105 years, compared to eternity, our time on this earth is short. James 4:14 (NIV) says, "Why, you do not even know what will happen tomorrow. What is your life? You are a mist that appears for a little while and then vanishes." Have you ever been in weather cold enough that you could see your breath? A puff of air that you could see for just a second and then it was gone—that's how James describes our life on this earth. It's just a puff and then it's gone. This chapter isn't written to cause you to become scared or worried about your life or death. It's written to help you, and me, become more aware of living a life of value. As teens, we are nearing adulthood. Our time as children is almost gone. It's weird to think of that, isn't it? But it's true. Already we're seeing that time is fleeting. So, start today being purposeful about the days you have on this earth.

This week I will seek to live more purposefully by

. . . . . . . . . . . . . . . . . . . . . . . . . . . . . . . . . . . . . . . . . . . . . . . . . . . . . . . . . . . . . . . . . . . . . . . . . . . . . .

. . . . . . . . . . . . . . . . . . . . . . . . . . . . . . . . . . . . . . . . . . . . . . . . . . . . . . . . . . . . . . . . . . . . . . . . . . . . . .

. . . . . . . . . . . . . . . . . . . . . . . . . . . . . . . . . . . . . . . . . . . . . . . . . . . . . . . . . . . . . . . . . . . . . . . . . . . . . .

. . . . . . . . . . . . . . . . . . . . . . . . . . . . . . . . . . . . . . . . . . . . . . . . . . . . . . . . . . . . . . . . . . . . . . . . . . . . . .

## Feelings Sometimes Feel Bad

I'VE BEEN VERY BLESSED to have not had many traumatic days. Having said that, none of us will go through life without some sad times. A few years ago my aunt and uncle decided to get a divorce. This was a very sad time for our family. Like most divorce situations, we loved everyone involved and didn't want to have to choose sides. Thankfully, we didn't have to choose since the adults never asked us to, so we were able to just be kids and love everyone. Still, we were sad that a part of our family was separating. Some of you have been through divorce in your family. Some of you have experienced the death of someone close to you, perhaps even your mom or dad or a sibling. Some of you might be experiencing the pain that goes along with losing your home. Bad things happen to good people all the time, and it's hard to be happy when there is so much to be sad about.

Emotions are good things—even the sad ones. God gave them to us, but we have to be careful with them. Some feelings or emotions are grounded in real things, and some can be deceptive. We can't let our feelings or emotions convince us that something that isn't reality is true. For example, we can "feel" like that cute new boy at school has a crush on us, but those feelings may have nothing to do with reality. Here's another example. We can "feel" like our mom or dad or a coach or a teacher is mad at us, but until we have a discussion with them, we don't know if it's true or not. For even bigger issues, like a divorce, we can feel like our life is falling apart, but there is always hope and God will be with us even in the darkest times.

Our teen years are full of emotional ups and downs. When things seem to be out of control, stay grounded by leaning on what you know to be true, not what you feel like is true.

## What Does the Bible Say about It?

**Psalm 119:105 (NIV)**
*Your word is a lamp for my feet, a light on my path.*

## Dig a Little Deeper

Have you ever tried to walk through a garage in the dark? It's nearly impossible without running into something and getting hurt. When we go through life without reading God's Word, it will be very hard to keep from getting hurt. Fill in this blank:

Psalm 119:105 *tells us that God's Word is a* . . . . . . . . . . . . . *on our path.*

In other words, God's Word is our flashlight to help get through the dark garage of life. Many books in the Bible are full of instructions for us to live so we can avoid disaster. Psalm 119 is the longest single chapter in the Bible, with 176 verses. It was written to encourage the reader, which is you, to live a life according to God's will, and when we live according to His will, it's easier to get through tough days. Notice I didn't say you wouldn't have tough days. I just said you would be able to handle them in a better way—it'll be easier to keep your emotions in check. Let's look at a few more "flashlight" verses that help shine the light during dark days.

Read Psalm 119:1–2 (NIV) and fill in the blanks.

.......................... are those whose ways are .................., who walk according to the law of the ................... Blessed are those who keep his statutes and .................. him with all their ......................

Read Psalm 119:9 (NIV) and fill in the blanks.

How can a young person stay on the path of ..................? By living .......................... to your word.

Read Psalm 199:76 (NIV) and fill in the blanks.

May your unfailing .................. be my .................., according to your .................. to your servant.

Psalm 119 is a great chapter to read when the events in your life seem out of order. It tells us that our God is a God of order and He is the only one who can bring order to a chaotic world.

## Live It!

Think about this example. The teacher is yelling at the entire class, but one student is deeply affected, believing the teacher hates her. That feeling takes root and everything that happens is filtered through this feeling that her teacher hates her. The teacher has never done anything to verify that she hates the student.

Have you ever had an experience similar to this example?

. . . . . . . . . . . . . . . . . . . . . . . . . . . . . . . . . . . . . . . . . . . . .

. . . . . . . . . . . . . . . . . . . . . . . . . . . . . . . . . . . . . . . . . . . . .

. . . . . . . . . . . . . . . . . . . . . . . . . . . . . . . . . . . . . . . . . . . . .

. . . . . . . . . . . . . . . . . . . . . . . . . . . . . . . . . . . . . . . . . . . . .

It's important that as we mature we learn to separate feelings from facts. Feelings cannot be trusted, but facts can. When we get stuck in a bad place where feelings are controlling our actions, we must do what we can to find out the facts. If this student had stayed after class to talk to the teacher, she might have discovered that the teacher doesn't hate her at all and a lot of hard feelings could have been avoided. Once you have found the facts, go to the Word of

God for guidance and direction. Go back and read the verses in Psalms and know that God is in control.

This week I will not let my feelings get in the way of

. . . . . . . . . . . . . . . . . . . . . . . . . . . . . . . . . . . . . . . . . . . . . . . . . .

. . . . . . . . . . . . . . . . . . . . . . . . . . . . . . . . . . . . . . . . . . . . . . . . . .

. . . . . . . . . . . . . . . . . . . . . . . . . . . . . . . . . . . . . . . . . . . . . . . . . .

. . . . . . . . . . . . . . . . . . . . . . . . . . . . . . . . . . . . . . . . . . . . . . . . . .

## Finish Strong

RAISE YOUR HAND if you like starting something new better than finishing it. My hand is up! New beginnings are such fun.

Now I'm not a big "I love school" person, but I do love the start of the school year. I love a new batch of pencils and fresh, clean notebooks and, of course, back-to-school shopping. (Who doesn't like that?) And I love seeing everyone I haven't seen in nearly three months. It's exciting to anticipate the fun I'll have with my friends at school. It's even fun to think about all the new things I'll learn. (Okay, the word "fun" might be a stretch here, but you get the point.)

Often we put a lot of emphasis on the beginning of an activity, but as the activity goes on, our best efforts fade away. Maybe we get bored or tired or lose interest. I don't know why this happens; I just know it does. And it's not a good thing. Nowhere in the Bible do we see an example of beginning something and then walking away from it. Walking away, or even slowing down, will never produce good results. We don't have to reach far into the Bible (see Genesis 6) to find the story of Noah and how seriously he took his job of building the ark. He followed God's instructions and didn't stop until every detail was perfect and the boat was ready to float.

One of my favorite movies is *Unbroken*. It's the true story of war hero Louis Zamperini. Everything about that man is inspirational, and I encourage you to read the book or see the movie. When Louis was asked about his many accomplishments, he said that one thing he learned from being a runner was to never give up, to fight to the finish. As an athlete I can relate to this. I've played on winning teams and losing teams, but I've never played on a team where I was coached to give up. All coaches teach their athletes to fight to the finish because they know that fighting hard, whether they win or lose, will make the players better people.

## What Does the Bible Say about It?

**Acts 20:24 (NIV)**
*However, I consider my life worth nothing to me; my only aim is to finish the race and complete the task the Lord Jesus has given me—the task of testifying to the good news of God's grace.*

## Dig a Little Deeper

The book of Acts was written by Luke, who was a follower of Jesus.

Read Acts 1:1 and Luke 1:3. Who did Luke write both of these books to?

.................................................................

.................................................................

.................................................................

In my research, I found that no one knows much about Theophilus. But in the book of Luke we learn about the life of Jesus Christ, and the book of Acts tells the story of the apostles and how they carried out Jesus' command to preach the gospel. In Acts 20, Paul asks the elders from the city of Ephesus to come see him so he can say his good-byes to them.

Where does Paul tell the elders he is going next? (Acts 20:22)

.................................................................

.................................................................

.................................................................

What has the Holy Spirit warned Paul that he will encounter? (Acts 20:23)

.................................................................

.................................................................

.................................................................

How willing would you be to go someplace where you would surely face trouble?

.................................................................

.................................................................

What is Paul's only aim? (Acts 20:24)

. . . . . . . . . . . . . . . . . . . . . . . . . . . . . . . . . . . . . . . . . . . . . . . . . . . . . . . . . . . . .

. . . . . . . . . . . . . . . . . . . . . . . . . . . . . . . . . . . . . . . . . . . . . . . . . . . . . . . . . . . . .

. . . . . . . . . . . . . . . . . . . . . . . . . . . . . . . . . . . . . . . . . . . . . . . . . . . . . . . . . . . . .

## Live It!

Recently I was asked to be in a movie about the life of Rachel Scott. Rachel was killed on April 20, 1999, during a shooting at her school, Columbine High School, in Littleton, Colorado. As I was preparing for my part in the movie, I read about her life and death. Rachel was an amazing girl who loved to act and write. She was a normal seventeen-year-old with hopes and dreams for a future. Her life was cut short when two troubled guys killed twelve students and a teacher at her high school. She was the first one to die. Her friend Richard was the first one shot. They were enjoying a beautiful day eating their lunch outside when the shooters approached them.

Soon after the shooting, Richard told his mom that the shooters asked Rachel if she believed in God. Her answer was, "You know I do." And then they killed her.

Standing up for God in the face of death is the ultimate "finishing strong." It's something most of us cannot even imagine. On page 110 of the book *The Journals of Rachel Scott*, Rachel says: "Don't give up, because God's reward is worth it all. Whatever it takes, do it. Seek God with a whole heart. Love God with a passion. And don't give the excuse, 'I am just a teenager . . .'" She goes on to say more and ends her thoughts with these important words, "Christianity is not a label, but a lifestyle."

I don't even know how to end this "Live It!" section. Rachel's story gives me a deeper perspective, and I hope it does for you too. If you haven't totally dedicated your life to Jesus Christ, today is the day to do that. Go to a youth leader or a friend who is on fire for God, and they will help guide you.

## Ready, Set, Grow!

Today I will make plans to finish strong by

. . . . . . . . . . . . . . . . . . . . . . . . . . . . . . . . . . . . . . . . . . . . . . . . . . . . . . . . . .

. . . . . . . . . . . . . . . . . . . . . . . . . . . . . . . . . . . . . . . . . . . . . . . . . . . . . . . . . .

. . . . . . . . . . . . . . . . . . . . . . . . . . . . . . . . . . . . . . . . . . . . . . . . . . . . . . . . . .

. . . . . . . . . . . . . . . . . . . . . . . . . . . . . . . . . . . . . . . . . . . . . . . . . . . . . . . . . .

*Friends Forever*

I LOVE MY FRIENDS! True friends, forever friends, are like spiritual gifts from God. They are there to support you in good times and bad times.

Like everything else in life, God lets us choose our friends. Even our parents can't choose our friends for us. Maybe your first friend lived close to you. Maybe she was in gymnastics with you. We are usually attracted to people who have similar interests. There are many reasons we choose our first friendships.

But relationships, just like people, change. This is a part of life. A friend you had in elementary school might not be such a good friend in high school. This might make you sad, but as we get older, we have different ideas and experiences that shape who we are..

But what happens when friends start to hang out with people who are a bad influence on them? That puts you in a tough spot. Do you confront them? Do you still hang out with them and try to remind them of who they used to be?

I say yes and yes. If you're worried about your friends, pray for them. Then, go to them and tell them your worries, but don't expect them to be willing to change right then. First, they might be embarrassed, and pride might get in the way of them seeing that you are trying to help them. Second, they might not want to change. Your friends might be happy right where they are, thank you very much. Once you have done everything you can do, you might have to limit your time with that person, but increase the time you pray for them.

When we talk about forever friends, we talk about friends who will spend eternity with us. Just because your friend is struggling right now doesn't mean that friend is forever lost. Two-Mama loves Facebook because she gets to see how her friends from high school are now living for God. Even if you can't hang out with a friend who is walking a bad path, you can still be kind and friendly to her. You can let her know she is loved, and you can pray for her.

Most important, stay true to who you are. The best way to influence others is by example. I love watching my friends serve God on social media, like my grandma does with her friends, but I really look forward to spending eternity with them.

What Does the Bible Say about It?

**Proverbs 17:17 (NIV)**
*A friend loves at all times.*

This is such a simple verse, but it is very powerful. The word that makes it powerful is the word "all." Some synonyms for "all" are "completely," "totally," and "wholly." Most of the time, our friendships are based on conditions, such as "If you do this or act this way, then I will like you." Let's look at some other scriptures that will help us understand how to be a good friend.

Read Proverbs 14:30. What kind of heart is the best to have?

. . . . . . . . . . . . . . . . . . . . . . . . . . . . . . . . . . . . . . . . . . . . . . . . . . . . .

. . . . . . . . . . . . . . . . . . . . . . . . . . . . . . . . . . . . . . . . . . . . . . . . . . . . .

. . . . . . . . . . . . . . . . . . . . . . . . . . . . . . . . . . . . . . . . . . . . . . . . . . . . .

Read James 3:16. What two things can cause disorder?

. . . . . . . . . . . . . . . . . . . . . . . . . . . . . . . . . . . . . . . . . . . . . . . . . . . . .

. . . . . . . . . . . . . . . . . . . . . . . . . . . . . . . . . . . . . . . . . . . . . . . . . . . . .

. . . . . . . . . . . . . . . . . . . . . . . . . . . . . . . . . . . . . . . . . . . . . . . . . . . . .

Read Philippians 2:3–4. Write this verse in your own words.

. . . . . . . . . . . . . . . . . . . . . . . . . . . . . . . . . . . . . . . . . . . . . . . . . . . . .

. . . . . . . . . . . . . . . . . . . . . . . . . . . . . . . . . . . . . . . . . . . . . . . . . . . . .

. . . . . . . . . . . . . . . . . . . . . . . . . . . . . . . . . . . . . . . . . . . . . . . . . . . . .

Live It!

It's very hard to lose a friend. The reason for the loss might not even be a bad reason. You might just have different interests at different times in your life, but it's still hard. If you think of all of your friends as forever friends, the transition will be easier. In other words, continue to pray for your friends and check on them from time to time. Let them know that just because you don't hang out on a regular basis doesn't mean you don't care about them and love them. A simple note or text saying you're thinking about them will go a long way toward keeping the bond strong. After all, your goal in life is to spend eternity with them, not just a few years in high school.

🦋 Ready, Set, Grow! 🦋

This week, I will pray for

. . . . . . . . . . . . . . . . . . . . . . . . . . . . . . . . . . . . . . . . . . . . . . . . . . . . . . .

. . . . . . . . . . . . . . . . . . . . . . . . . . . . . . . . . . . . . . . . . . . . . . . . . . . . . . .

. . . . . . . . . . . . . . . . . . . . . . . . . . . . . . . . . . . . . . . . . . . . . . . . . . . . . . .

. . . . . . . . . . . . . . . . . . . . . . . . . . . . . . . . . . . . . . . . . . . . . . . . . . . . . . .

# Five Seconds of Awkward

M Y COUSIN KATELYN gave me some great advice that I want to pass on to you. Katelyn is my older cousin and has two little boys. She's a great role model for me. One night several of my friends were at Katelyn's house for a Bible study. We were talking about what to do when we find ourselves in a situation that is not right. Maybe your "friends" pull out the beer, or your boyfriend's hand goes where it's not supposed to go, or hateful gossip is the topic of conversation. You know those situations. Awkward, right? So what do you do?

Katelyn's advice was, "Five seconds of awkward can save you a lifetime of regret." Brilliant! All of us will have those moments when one wrong decision will cause deep hurt and regret. Even the smallest thing we do each day can have good or bad consequences. It's like what we learn in physics (or should have learned): every action has an equal and opposite reaction. That means everything we do will affect someone or something. Like a wave in the ocean, our actions will have a ripple effect.

So many times teens want to say, "It's my life. It shouldn't bother anyone else." But "it," whatever "it" is, always does. That's how life works. One word or action can change the path you're on. That's why the five-seconds-of-awkward rule is so great. If we are willing to be awkward for just five seconds, we can move forward on a good path. Standing up for what we believe won't always be easy, but it will always be right.

What Does the Bible Say about It?

**1 Timothy 4:12 (NIV)**
*Don't let anyone look down on you because you are young, but set an example for the believers in speech, in conduct, in love, in faith and in purity.*

Dig a Little Deeper

The apostle Paul wrote the book of 1 Timothy to help churches in their leadership and organization. If you want to know about elders and deacons and how people are to conduct themselves during worship time, this is your book. By the time Paul wrote 1 Timothy, he was an older man and Timothy was a young preacher. Paul knew that since Timothy was young he might not get the respect he deserved. Paul knew Timothy might have a few five-seconds-of-awkward moments as he stood up for what was right.

Let's first look at where Paul meets this young man named Timothy. Read Acts 16:1–3.

What city did Timothy live in?

. . . . . . . . . . . . . . . . . . . . . . . . . . . . . . . . . . . . . . . . . . . . . . . . . . . . . . . .

. . . . . . . . . . . . . . . . . . . . . . . . . . . . . . . . . . . . . . . . . . . . . . . . . . . . . . . .

What does this verse say about Timothy's parents?

. . . . . . . . . . . . . . . . . . . . . . . . . . . . . . . . . . . . . . . . . . . . . . . . . . . . . . . .

. . . . . . . . . . . . . . . . . . . . . . . . . . . . . . . . . . . . . . . . . . . . . . . . . . . . . . . .

. . . . . . . . . . . . . . . . . . . . . . . . . . . . . . . . . . . . . . . . . . . . . . . . . . . . . . . .

What did Paul hear about Timothy that made him want to travel with him?

. . . . . . . . . . . . . . . . . . . . . . . . . . . . . . . . . . . . . . . . . . . . . . . . . . . . . . . .

. . . . . . . . . . . . . . . . . . . . . . . . . . . . . . . . . . . . . . . . . . . . . . . . . . . . . . . .

. . . . . . . . . . . . . . . . . . . . . . . . . . . . . . . . . . . . . . . . . . . . . . . . . . . . . . . .

In 1 Timothy 4:12 Paul tells Timothy to not let anyone look down on him because he is young.

Write about a time when you felt like you were not heard because of your age or some other reason.

. . . . . . . . . . . . . . . . . . . . . . . . . . . . . . . . . . . . . . . . . . . . . . . . . . . . . . . .

. . . . . . . . . . . . . . . . . . . . . . . . . . . . . . . . . . . . . . . . . . . . . . . . . . . . . . . .

. . . . . . . . . . . . . . . . . . . . . . . . . . . . . . . . . . . . . . . . . . . . . . . . . . . . . . . .

List five things Paul says we should be an example in.

1. . . . . . . . . . . . . . . . . . . . . . . . . . . . . . . . . . . . . . . . . . . . . . . . . . . . . . .

2. . . . . . . . . . . . . . . . . . . . . . . . . . . . . . . . . . . . . . . . . . . . . . . . . . . . . . .

3. . . . . . . . . . . . . . . . . . . . . . . . . . . . . . . . . . . . . . . . . . . . . . . . . . . . . . .

4. . . . . . . . . . . . . . . . . . . . . . . . . . . . . . . . . . . . . . . . . . . . . . . . . . . . . . . . . . . . .

5. . . . . . . . . . . . . . . . . . . . . . . . . . . . . . . . . . . . . . . . . . . . . . . . . . . . . . . . . . . . .

## Live It!

Knowing and doing are two different things. I know how to load the dishwasher, but it's rare that I want to do it, right? After today's lesson you know that every action you take will have a reaction—a consequence—an outcome. Again, these aren't always bad. They are just a fact of life. If I brush my teeth every day, I will have healthier teeth. That's an action with a good outcome and a good consequence. But many situations we find ourselves in require a quick no-more-than-five-seconds response that could put us on a path we don't want to go on. The good news is it could set a positive example for others.

What awkward moment have you had to face?

. . . . . . . . . . . . . . . . . . . . . . . . . . . . . . . . . . . . . . . . . . . . . . . . . . . . . . . . . . . .

. . . . . . . . . . . . . . . . . . . . . . . . . . . . . . . . . . . . . . . . . . . . . . . . . . . . . . . . . . . .

. . . . . . . . . . . . . . . . . . . . . . . . . . . . . . . . . . . . . . . . . . . . . . . . . . . . . . . . . . . .

. . . . . . . . . . . . . . . . . . . . . . . . . . . . . . . . . . . . . . . . . . . . . . . . . . . . . . . . . . . .

How will this lesson help you face future dilemmas?

. . . . . . . . . . . . . . . . . . . . . . . . . . . . . . . . . . . . . . . . . . . . . . . . . . . . . . . . . . . .

. . . . . . . . . . . . . . . . . . . . . . . . . . . . . . . . . . . . . . . . . . . . . . . . . . . . . . . . . . . .

. . . . . . . . . . . . . . . . . . . . . . . . . . . . . . . . . . . . . . . . . . . . . . . . . . . . . . . . . . . .

. . . . . . . . . . . . . . . . . . . . . . . . . . . . . . . . . . . . . . . . . . . . . . . . . . . . . . . . . . . .

Here is my five-second pledge. You can write it on a note-card or put it in your phone. Use it to help you get through any awkward moments.

I will stand up for my beliefs and I will do what's right, no matter what. I'll stand strong against temptation and peer pressure. God has an amazing future planned for me, and I won't let five seconds of awkward ruin a lifetime of awesome.

⚘ Ready, Set, Grow! ⚘

This week I will practice the five-second rule by

. . . . . . . . . . . . . . . . . . . . . . . . . . . . . . . . . . . . . . . . . . . . . . . . . . . . .

. . . . . . . . . . . . . . . . . . . . . . . . . . . . . . . . . . . . . . . . . . . . . . . . . . . . .

. . . . . . . . . . . . . . . . . . . . . . . . . . . . . . . . . . . . . . . . . . . . . . . . . . . . .

. . . . . . . . . . . . . . . . . . . . . . . . . . . . . . . . . . . . . . . . . . . . . . . . . . . . .

## Garbage In, Garbage Out

THE PHRASE "GARBAGE IN, GARBAGE OUT" (GIGO) was first used in the computer world. Twenty years ago my Uncle Jeremy was the first to teach computer science in the school I now attend. Those early computers were big boxes set on top of the desks, and they were bulky and awkward compared to what we use today. Even though they were bigger, they held less information.

Uncle Jeremy says he taught his computer programming students the "garbage in, garbage out" principle as one of his first lessons. Simply put, the quality of output is determined by the quality of input. For example, if you put the wrong math facts in a computer, you won't get the right answer. As great as computers are, they are dependent on what their programmers put in them.

This principle is true for people too. Our brains are complicated, amazing, supercomplex, highly sophisticated computers. God did all the wiring, so—on top of all that—they are perfect. But they operate on the GIGO principle. God chose not to create us as robots that think and act alike. God wants our actions to be out of a decision to love Him. He doesn't want our obedience to be programmed in.

Did you ever have a talking doll? You know, the ones that say "I love you" or "Will you play with me?" when you push a button or pull a string. My grandma Two-Mama has one of the original Chatty Cathy dolls. Two-Mama says she loved that doll and loved to hear it talk to her. In reality, Chatty Cathy could only say the eleven phrases someone put into her on the production line. Today Chatty Cathy sits on top of a shelf, looking pretty good, but she has lost her voice.

Our God didn't want to give us eleven things to say in random order. He loves to hear us say words that bring glory to Him and show respect for others. He loves to watch us do things that honor His creation and reflect the good in this world. But for that to happen, we have to be disciplined about what goes into our minds. If you fill your mind with negative thoughts, bad words, or ideas that are not nice or respectful toward others, you will eventually think bad thoughts, use bad language, and act on bad ideas. The opposite is also true. When you fill you mind with positive thoughts, good words, and ideas that are pure and respectful toward others, you will soon think good thoughts, use good language, and act on good ideas.

**Proverbs 4:23 (NIV)**

*Above all else, guard your heart, for everything you do flows from it.*

 Dig a Little Deeper

The verse above is from the New International Version, which many now use as their main Bible source. But sometimes it's interesting to look at other translations. Let's look at a few more translations of Proverbs 4:23.

**New Living Translation (NLT)**

*Guard your heart above all else, for it determines the course of your life.*

**King James Version (KJV)**

*Keep thy heart with all diligence; for out of it are the issues of life.*

**International Standard Version (ISV)**

*Above everything else guard your heart, because from it flow the springs of life.*

Each version is worded a little differently, but all of them tell us to protect our hearts. We know that as long as our physical hearts are functioning properly, we are alive. Our physical hearts have to be cared for with good food and exercise. But this verse isn't about our physical heart. This verse is about our spiritual heart.

What are some ways you could protect your spiritual heart?

. . . . . . . . . . . . . . . . . . . . . . . . . . . . . . . . . . . . . . . . . . . . . . . . . . . . . . . . .

. . . . . . . . . . . . . . . . . . . . . . . . . . . . . . . . . . . . . . . . . . . . . . . . . . . . . . . . .

. . . . . . . . . . . . . . . . . . . . . . . . . . . . . . . . . . . . . . . . . . . . . . . . . . . . . . . . .

Read Mark 14:38 (NIV) and fill in the blanks below.

. . . . . . . . . . . . . . . . . . *and* . . . . . . . . . . . . . . . . . . . *so that you will not fall into temptation. The spirit is willing, but the flesh is weak.*

What two things did you find that you can do to protect your heart?

. . . . . . . . . . . . . . . . . . . . . . . . . *and* . . . . . . . . . . . . . . . . . . . . . . . . .

Live It!

The last scripture we read gives us great insight into how we can protect our hearts. It says to watch and pray. Sometimes, especially as teens, we go about our day waiting for the phone to ring or a text to come that tells us what we will do that day. Sometimes we say "yes" to things we don't even think through.

Why do we do that?

. . . . . . . . . . . . . . . . . . . . . . . . . . . . . . . . . . . . . . . . . . . . . . . . . . . . . . . . .

. . . . . . . . . . . . . . . . . . . . . . . . . . . . . . . . . . . . . . . . . . . . . . . . . . . . . . . . .

If we would take a minute to think about—or, as this verse says, "watch"—what we are about to do or say or see, it would make a huge difference. This verse also says to pray. Once again, if we stop and pray before jumping into something that could be harmful, the outcome would be very different. Let's keep the letters GIGO, but change the phrase from "garbage in, garbage out" to "Godly in, Godly out." If we can do that, we allow only the things that will move us to greatness through God into our hearts.

### ❧ Ready, Set, Grow! ❧

This week I will pledge to only let Godly things in by

. . . . . . . . . . . . . . . . . . . . . . . . . . . . . . . . . . . . . . . . . . . . . . . . . . . . . . . . . . . . .

. . . . . . . . . . . . . . . . . . . . . . . . . . . . . . . . . . . . . . . . . . . . . . . . . . . . . . . . . . . . .

. . . . . . . . . . . . . . . . . . . . . . . . . . . . . . . . . . . . . . . . . . . . . . . . . . . . . . . . . . . . .

. . . . . . . . . . . . . . . . . . . . . . . . . . . . . . . . . . . . . . . . . . . . . . . . . . . . . . . . . . . . .

## Grow Up Great

IN MY BOOK *LIVE ORIGINAL*, I say that I want to grow up great. I know. It's a pretty big goal and not very specific. So more specifically, I want to accomplish great things and be someone who makes a positive difference in the world around me. I added those last words, "around me," for a reason. The fact that my family now has a TV show and our outreach is bigger hasn't changed who we are. When I look at all my bearded uncles and beautiful aunts, I see them doing exactly what they were doing before the show, only now they have a larger audience. Don't wait until you have a platform or bigger audience to be great. Be great and you will have a platform.

Years ago, my Uncle Alan and Aunt Lisa went through a difficult time in their marriage. Since then they have helped others who are struggling to find love again and repair their broken marriages. My Uncle Jason and Aunt Missy have always been involved with the youth at our church. In the summer Aunt Missy heads up the arts and crafts program at our local camp, and Uncle Jason speaks to the campers about sharing the good news of Jesus. Papaw Phil and Mamaw Kay have always opened their home to anyone for a meal and a message about Jesus. These are just a few examples of how my family serves God. I am blessed to see great men and women whose greatness doesn't come from being on a TV show, but from a desire to serve God.

One time when John Luke spoke to a large crowd, he encouraged them to start at the end of their life and work backward. In other words, see yourself as you want to be when you're eighty, and then think about what it would take to be that person. Do you want to be someone who is kind and strong and who makes others smile? Then be that person now. Do you want to be wise and thoughtful and give advice that helps others lead a good life? Do it now. Do you want to sing on a worship team and lead others in worship? Find your place now.

Being great doesn't depend on the circumstances around you—it depends on YOU.

## What Does the Bible Say about It?

### Colossians 1:10 (NIV)

*. . . so that you may live a life worthy of the Lord and please him in every way: bearing fruit in every good work, growing in the knowledge of God . . .*

Read Colossians 1:1. Who wrote the book of Colossians?

. . . . . . . . . . . . . . . . . . . . . . . . . . . . . . . . . . . . . . . . . . . . . . . . . . . .

. . . . . . . . . . . . . . . . . . . . . . . . . . . . . . . . . . . . . . . . . . . . . . . . . . . .

. . . . . . . . . . . . . . . . . . . . . . . . . . . . . . . . . . . . . . . . . . . . . . . . . . . .

Read Colossians 1:2. Who is he writing this letter to?

. . . . . . . . . . . . . . . . . . . . . . . . . . . . . . . . . . . . . . . . . . . . . . . . . . . .

. . . . . . . . . . . . . . . . . . . . . . . . . . . . . . . . . . . . . . . . . . . . . . . . . . . .

. . . . . . . . . . . . . . . . . . . . . . . . . . . . . . . . . . . . . . . . . . . . . . . . . . . .

For others to hear the good news of Jesus, someone else must be willing to share. Who shared with the people in Colossae? (Colossians 1:7)

. . . . . . . . . . . . . . . . . . . . . . . . . . . . . . . . . . . . . . . . . . . . . . . . . . . .

. . . . . . . . . . . . . . . . . . . . . . . . . . . . . . . . . . . . . . . . . . . . . . . . . . . .

. . . . . . . . . . . . . . . . . . . . . . . . . . . . . . . . . . . . . . . . . . . . . . . . . . . .

Paul wanted the Christians in Colossae to understand what Jesus had done for them. Read Colossians 1:15. How does Paul describe Jesus?

. . . . . . . . . . . . . . . . . . . . . . . . . . . . . . . . . . . . . . . . . . . . . . . . . . . .

. . . . . . . . . . . . . . . . . . . . . . . . . . . . . . . . . . . . . . . . . . . . . . . . . . . .

. . . . . . . . . . . . . . . . . . . . . . . . . . . . . . . . . . . . . . . . . . . . . . . . . . . .

Paul presented a Jesus who is not only the creator of the universe and the Savior of the world, but also supreme over all creation. Truly understanding who Jesus is should be a call to action. It should leave us with the desire to grow and become great by God's standards, not by the world's standards.

Notice how the verse Colossians 1:10 is printed several pages earlier. It begins and ends with an ellipsis. An ellipsis is written with three dots. This indicates there is more to read on either side of this statement. In other words, Colossians 1:10 is not a complete thought. To read the complete thought, read verses 9–12.

## Live It!

Some experts say it takes ten thousand hours of practice to be really good at something. Isn't that crazy? We all want to think that athletes, musicians, actors, magicians, and other "great" people are just naturals at what they do. Believing this might make it easier to be jealous. The truth is everyone has to work hard at whatever they want to be. If you want to grow up to be great, you have to start now. From the time I was little, I knew I wanted to teach others about Jesus. There's a video floating around in cyberspace of me preaching when I was about five years old. That was my humble beginning. As I got older I looked for opportunities to share my faith. Sometimes I only had an audience of two—my mom and Two-Mama. But I kept working, and before I knew it, I was speaking to a crowd of ten thousand at Winter Jam.

What do you want to be great at? (Remember, it can range from being kind to others to winning *American Idol*. It takes all kinds to make a world, and your light can shine anywhere and anytime.)

. . . . . . . . . . . . . . . . . . . . . . . . . . . . . . . . . . . . . . . . . . . . . . .

. . . . . . . . . . . . . . . . . . . . . . . . . . . . . . . . . . . . . . . . . . . . . . .

. . . . . . . . . . . . . . . . . . . . . . . . . . . . . . . . . . . . . . . . . . . . . . .

Take that first step this week toward accomplishing that goal.

### ⁖ Ready, Set, Grow! ⁖

This week I will take the first steps toward being great at . . . . . . . . . . . . . . . . . . . . . . . . . by . . . . . . . . . . . . . . . . . . . . . . . . . .

*Give It Up for God*

REMEMBER THAT PREACHING VIDEO of me when I was five years old that's floating around somewhere on the Internet? You can probably find it on YouTube. This was the start of my preaching career. I would stand in front of the fireplace at my house or my grandparents' house and preach to anyone who would listen. I had actually forgotten I used to preach like that until my sixteenth birthday party.

My mom decided turning sixteen was going to be a big deal, so after weeks of planning, about 150 friends and family members walked the "Redneck Red Carpet" at my sweet sixteen birthday party. It was so much fun. My mom had arranged for two special friends, the Junk Gypsies, to decorate, and she got Scotty McCreery to come sing. I couldn't have asked for a better birthday party. But there was one surprise no one knew about. My Two-Papa (Mom's daddy) had saved that video of me preaching and had arranged to project it on a big screen during the night of my party.

At the end of the party, Two-Papa called everyone together and told us he had a surprise. (If your grandpa is like my grandpa, you're not always thinking it's a good thing when he says there's a surprise). We all sat down on blanket-covered haystacks under the Louisiana summer sky and watched my little five-year-old self preaching the gospel on a movie screen made out of a giant sheet. It wasn't long before everyone was crying, including me. Seeing myself at such a young age was impactful, but hearing the words I was saying was especially meaningful. At one point I said, "Even if I become famous, it won't matter, I will still love God." Then I end my preaching session with an enthusiastic cheer, "Give it up for God!"

I'm so thankful that my Two-Papa thought to save that video and keep it close so it could remind me where my heart was at five years old. I love the innocence that comes with being five. Before sin enters our world, we can so confidently say, "Give it up for God." It seems easy to give it up for God when you've never lived through a friend dying, people saying hateful things about you, a parent leaving, friends who choose to take the wrong path, and a thousand other things that can change us by our sixteenth birthdays. But that's exactly when we *need* to say "Give it up for God" and really mean it. It's because of God we can walk through those tough days of life and still be able to cheer.

**Psalm 124:8 (NIV)**
*Our help is in the name of the LORD, the Maker of heaven and earth.*

───── Dig a Little Deeper ─────

I love this verse. I love all of Psalm 124. It's a short chapter, but a powerful one. Read 124:1–5 (NIV).

If God had not been with Israel when people attacked them, many bad things would have happened. See if you can name them.

1. .................................................... them alive.
2. The attackers would have .................... them alive.
3. ............................................ would have swept them away.

After David gives the description of bad things that could have happened to Israel, he pretty much says, "Give it up for God." Read Psalm 124:6–8 (NIV) and fill in the blanks.

*Praise be to the LORD, who has not let us be torn by their teeth. We have .................... like a bird from the fowler's snare; the .................... has been broken, and we have..................... Our help is in the name of the LORD, the .................... of heaven and earth.*

After telling all the mighty things God did for the Israelites, David says, "Our help is in the name of the Lord, the Maker of heaven and earth!" David is saying we need to raise the roof about our mighty God. Go God!!

## Live It!

The verse we are looking at this week is in Psalms. Do you remember that Psalms are songs? The cool thing about this Psalm is the message is still sung in churches today. We sing a version at my home church, and I love how it reminds me that God is on my side. You might want to check YouTube and listen to a version. The name of the song is "Had It Not Been for the Lord."

Can you name a time when you knew God was on your side, helping you through a hard time?

. . . . . . . . . . . . . . . . . . . . . . . . . . . . . . . . . . . . . . . . . . . . . . . . . . . .
. . . . . . . . . . . . . . . . . . . . . . . . . . . . . . . . . . . . . . . . . . . . . . . . . . . .
. . . . . . . . . . . . . . . . . . . . . . . . . . . . . . . . . . . . . . . . . . . . . . . . . . . .
. . . . . . . . . . . . . . . . . . . . . . . . . . . . . . . . . . . . . . . . . . . . . . . . . . . .

How do you "give it up for God"?

. . . . . . . . . . . . . . . . . . . . . . . . . . . . . . . . . . . . . . . . . . . . . . . . . . . .
. . . . . . . . . . . . . . . . . . . . . . . . . . . . . . . . . . . . . . . . . . . . . . . . . . . .
. . . . . . . . . . . . . . . . . . . . . . . . . . . . . . . . . . . . . . . . . . . . . . . . . . . .
. . . . . . . . . . . . . . . . . . . . . . . . . . . . . . . . . . . . . . . . . . . . . . . . . . . .

We cheer at many things in life. We even have cheerleaders help us cheer. Take a few minutes and write a cheer about God. Don't worry, it's okay if it sounds a little corny. God won't mind at all. Pretend you're five years old and "give it up for God!"

........................................................
........................................................
........................................................
........................................................

### ❧ Ready, Set, Grow! ❧

This week I'm going to let God know I love Him by

........................................................
........................................................
........................................................
........................................................

## Hurting People Need an ARK

M Y THREE MONTHS IN LOS ANGELES during the filming of *Dancing with the Stars* were truly life-changing in many ways. Don't ever think that I don't love West Monroe, Louisiana, because I do, but it was fun to live in a big city for a few months. It opened my eyes to many things. I learned that even big cities love God and there are some awesome churches in Los Angeles. I discovered that even a small light can shine brightly when there is darkness. I saw how God's beauty will shine through no matter what challenges man puts before Him. And I learned that there are hurting people everywhere.

Hurt goes beyond where you live. It goes beyond beautiful scenery and nice weather. And hurt is deepest when it's about relationships. From coast to coast, the hurting people I talk to tell me about their latest sickness or job loss, but mostly I hear about parents who are getting a divorce or best friends who are doing drugs or a family member who is living with someone who hurts them. People hurt with and for other people. You may be thinking you don't know how to help people in situations like these. This is a lie of the devil, because if you love God, you really can help someone.

All hurting people need an ARK. No, not the type of ark that Noah built. They need an Act of Random Kindness. What I love about an act of random kindness is that one act has the potential to show a hurting person they are not alone. One caring act can change someone's day or maybe even his or her life. You don't have to look far to see someone hurting. You don't have to go to a bigger city or another country. Hurting people are in your church family and at your school and in the parking lot at Walmart. You just have to keep your eyes open to see and your heart open to help.

## What Does the Bible Say about It?

**Colossians 3:12 (NIV)**
*Therefore, as God's chosen people, holy and dearly loved, clothe yourselves with compassion, kindness, humility, gentleness and patience.*

## Dig a Little Deeper

In an earlier lesson we looked at who wrote Colossians and who it was written to. I hope you understand that Paul was telling the believers in Colossae about his mighty Savior, Jesus. It's also important to understand why Paul needed to say these things.

Read Colossians 2:4. Why was Paul writing to them?

. . . . . . . . . . . . . . . . . . . . . . . . . . . . . . . . . . . . . . . . . . . . . . . . . . . . . . . . . .

. . . . . . . . . . . . . . . . . . . . . . . . . . . . . . . . . . . . . . . . . . . . . . . . . . . . . . . . . .

. . . . . . . . . . . . . . . . . . . . . . . . . . . . . . . . . . . . . . . . . . . . . . . . . . . . . . . . . .

It's easy for any of us to believe the lies Satan sends our way. That is why we have to constantly stay alert to Satan's evil ways and why we have to stay wrapped up in Jesus. Only when we are strong in the Lord can we reach out to other hurting people.

Colossians 3:12 says we are to . . . . . . . . . . . . . . . . . . . . . ourselves with five things. Name those five things.

1. . . . . . . . . . . . . . . . . . . . . . . . . . . . . . . . . . . . . . . . . . . . . . . . . . . . . . . . . . .

2. . . . . . . . . . . . . . . . . . . . . . . . . . . . . . . . . . . . . . . . . . . . . . . . . . . . . . . . . . .

3. . . . . . . . . . . . . . . . . . . . . . . . . . . . . . . . . . . . . . . . . . . . . . . . . . . . . . . . . . .

4. . . . . . . . . . . . . . . . . . . . . . . . . . . . . . . . . . . . . . . . . . . . . . . . . . . . . . . . . . .

5. . . . . . . . . . . . . . . . . . . . . . . . . . . . . . . . . . . . . . . . . . . . . . . . . . . . . . . . . . .

I love that Paul used the word "clothe." That's a word we can all understand because we spend lots of our time talking about, shopping for, and changing clothes. We get it that Paul means for us to be totally wrapped up in those five character traits.

Each of the character traits in Colossians 3:12 are traits directed toward others. Think about it. There's not one mention of things that are directed just for our own growth, like silent meditation or alone time in the garden. There are other scriptures that tell us that's important too, but in this book, a book directed at believing people who need instructions on living, God says the most important thing is to treat others with kindness and gentleness. God knows we will grow the most when we are doing something for others. Look around for a time when you can share an ARK. I promise, you won't have to look far. You might want to hand a homeless person a sack of food, or you might notice a young mom trying to balance a baby and a shopping cart in need of someone to step in and help by pushing her cart. Yes, a random act of kindness is random, but some planning has to be involved. Plan today to find someone to help.

### Ready, Set, Grow!

This week I will be more mindful of hurting people and will

. . . . . . . . . . . . . . . . . . . . . . . . . . . . . . . . . . . . . . . . . . . . . . . . . . . . . . . .

. . . . . . . . . . . . . . . . . . . . . . . . . . . . . . . . . . . . . . . . . . . . . . . . . . . . . . . .

. . . . . . . . . . . . . . . . . . . . . . . . . . . . . . . . . . . . . . . . . . . . . . . . . . . . . . . .

. . . . . . . . . . . . . . . . . . . . . . . . . . . . . . . . . . . . . . . . . . . . . . . . . . . . . . . .

## Heaven Bound

DON'T THINK we spend enough time talking about Heaven, yet this is our real home! At my church we sing a song that says, "This world is not my home, I'm just passing through." For most of us, for most of the time, we live like this earth is our final destination. But it's not.

Life on this earth can be awesome for sure. I love to sit around a fire pit with my cousins and just talk and laugh, I love to climb in my bed after a busy day and snuggle with my sister, I love to go to the beach and have nothing to do but soak up the sun, I love to dance in the living room and watch my dad try a few dance moves, I love pizza and lobster and mountains covered in snow and friends and basketball and working out and Los Angeles and my family. But as much as I love all these things on earth, Heaven will be better.

A few years ago I read *Heaven is for Real*. It's the story of a little boy named Colton who had a near-death experience and saw a glimpse of Heaven. The book got a lot of attention. It's miracle kind of stuff, and there are some who do not believe Colton's story. But for me, reading it was a reminder of what I already know: Heaven IS for real and I want to go there. We won't all agree on specifics about Heaven because the Bible doesn't tell us everything. What we have to agree on is that Heaven is the place we all want to go to. If we accept Christ into our hearts, it's our final destination—our true home base.

I described the good parts of life on this earth, but let me describe a few of the bad parts. There are starving children, people addicted to drugs, violence and bloodshed, divorce, too much crime and hatred and abuse and loneliness and sadness and despair and impatience and depression. The song I mentioned earlier ends with these words: ". . . and I can't feel at home in this world anymore." If you believe that your true home is Heaven, you have to start living like you believe that. All the sadness of this world *needs us* to believe there is a better place. Keeping Heaven alive and making it real to ourselves and others will help us walk our walk on earth with more joy and peace.

## What Does the Bible Say about It?

**John 14:3 (NIV)**
*And if I go and prepare a place for you, I will come back and take you to be with me that you also may be where I am.*

I don't have all the answers about Heaven, but no one does. But we can know everything we *need* to know about it. God isn't a God of secrets, but it is up to us to read and study. You might be confused about something you're reading. If you read differing opinions on one topic, remember that God's Word never changes, but the person who reads it always does. In other words, God's Word is true and has lasted for centuries. The history, wisdom, advice, and instructions found in the Bible will not change. But each time you read the Bible you will see something you have never seen before and your life will be changed in some way.

Let's look at some more verses about Heaven and see what we find.

Read Revelation 21:4 (NIV) and fill in the blanks.

*He will wipe every.............from their eyes. There will be no more .............or.............or .............or............., for the old order of things has passed away.*

Read John 14:2 (NIV) and fill in the blanks.

*My Father's house has many ...................; if that were not so, would I have told you that I am going there to .............a place for you?*

Read 1 Corinthians 15:52 (NIV) and fill in the blanks.

*In a* ............., *in the* ............. *of an eye, at the last trumpet. For the* ............. *will sound, the dead will be* ............. *imperishable, and we will be* .............

Three things we learned in these verses:

1. There will be no tears or sorrow in Heaven.

2. Jesus is preparing a house for us.

3. Our bodies will be changed.

Live It!

Living like we believe Heaven is real means two things. First, that we are committed to telling others what we know—that Jesus came to earth to die on the cross for our sins so we can live eternally in Heaven, and He will return one day to take all those who believe with Him. This message is called the gospel. The word "gospel" means "good news," and this is really good news. And second, we have to act like we believe the good news is true.

**Read 1 Peter 3:14.**
*So then, dear friends, since you are looking forward to this, make every effort to be found spotless, blameless and at peace with him.*

Write down the three things we should strive to do since we are looking forward to Heaven as our home.

1. ...........................................................................

2. ...........................................................................

3. ...........................................................................

I urge you to look up as many scriptures as you can find and study about this amazing place. We google Disneyland or New York City or any other place we want to travel to, but we rarely google Heaven. This is a good week to google Heaven and act like it's the best destination ever. Because it is!

### ⚘ Ready, Set, Grow! ⚘

This week I will learn more about Heaven by

...........................................................................

...........................................................................

...........................................................................

...........................................................................

## It's All in Your Head

HAVE YOU EVER TOLD YOUR MOM something like, "That teacher doesn't like me," only to hear her say, "Oh, honey, that's not true, it's all in your head." It can get pretty annoying to have someone tell you it's in your head when you *know* it's happening for real! But the truth is, many things do start in your head.

The ability to think is a gift from God. He didn't create us to be robots. A robot can only do what it has been programmed to do. But a human can take a thought or idea and decide what to do with the information. Luke 12:48 tells us that to everyone who has been given much, much will be demanded. Our ability to think is one of those "much" situations. God has given us the ability to use our brains in mighty ways, so now we have a responsibility to protect that ability.

Your brain holds a lot of information. This information will be your resource to tap into as you navigate your adult life. But if you don't guard what gets put in your brain, it will be full of useless information or, worse, information that causes you to think negative or sinful thoughts. In the movies we watch, the magazines we read, and the voices we listen to, we have to be sure we are feeding our brain what it needs to live a life that glorifies God. There's a reason your mom says it's all in your head: because it is.

## What Does the Bible Say about It?

**Philippians 4:8 (NIV)**
*Finally, brothers and sisters, whatever is true, whatever is noble, whatever is right, whatever is pure, whatever is lovely, whatever is admirable—if anything is excellent or praiseworthy—think about such things.*

## Dig a Little Deeper

Read the first two verses in Philippians 1 and answer the following questions.

Who is this letter from?

. . . . . . . . . . . . . . . . . . . . . . . . . . . . . . . . . . . . . . . . . . . . . . . . . . . . . . . . . . . .

. . . . . . . . . . . . . . . . . . . . . . . . . . . . . . . . . . . . . . . . . . . . . . . . . . . . . . . . . . . .

. . . . . . . . . . . . . . . . . . . . . . . . . . . . . . . . . . . . . . . . . . . . . . . . . . . . . . . . . . . .

Who is it written to?

. . . . . . . . . . . . . . . . . . . . . . . . . . . . . . . . . . . . . . . . . . . . . . . . . . . . . . . . . . . .

. . . . . . . . . . . . . . . . . . . . . . . . . . . . . . . . . . . . . . . . . . . . . . . . . . . . . . . . . . . .

. . . . . . . . . . . . . . . . . . . . . . . . . . . . . . . . . . . . . . . . . . . . . . . . . . . . . . . . . . . .

Read verses 7 and 8 in the first chapter of Philippines. Why does Paul feel like the Christians in Philippi are special to him?

. . . . . . . . . . . . . . . . . . . . . . . . . . . . . . . . . . . . . . . . . . . . . . . . .

. . . . . . . . . . . . . . . . . . . . . . . . . . . . . . . . . . . . . . . . . . . . . . . . .

. . . . . . . . . . . . . . . . . . . . . . . . . . . . . . . . . . . . . . . . . . . . . . . . .

Paul spends his time in this letter encouraging Christians to live up to the life that Jesus Christ died for them to experience.

What is the first word in Philippians 4:8?

. . . . . . . . . . . . . . . . . . . . . . . . . . . . . . . . . . . . . . . . . . . . . . . . .

When someone says "finally" to you, what does that mean?

. . . . . . . . . . . . . . . . . . . . . . . . . . . . . . . . . . . . . . . . . . . . . . . . .

. . . . . . . . . . . . . . . . . . . . . . . . . . . . . . . . . . . . . . . . . . . . . . . . .

. . . . . . . . . . . . . . . . . . . . . . . . . . . . . . . . . . . . . . . . . . . . . . . . .

It is like Paul is saying, "Oh yeah, I have one more important thing to tell you." He had given lots of encouraging words about how to act, but in this verse, he talks about what Christians should think about. List those eight things.

1. . . . . . . . . . . . . . . . . . . . . . . . . . . . . . . . . . . . . . . . . . . . . . . .

2. . . . . . . . . . . . . . . . . . . . . . . . . . . . . . . . . . . . . . . . . . . . . . . .

3. . . . . . . . . . . . . . . . . . . . . . . . . . . . . . . . . . . . . . . . . . . . . . . .

4. . . . . . . . . . . . . . . . . . . . . . . . . . . . . . . . . . . . . . . . . . . . . . . .

5. . . . . . . . . . . . . . . . . . . . . . . . . . . . . . . . . . . . . . . . . . . . . . . .

6. . . . . . . . . . . . . . . . . . . . . . . . . . . . . . . . . . . . . . . . . . . . . . . .

7. . . . . . . . . . . . . . . . . . . . . . . . . . . . . . . . . . . . . . . . . . . . . . . . . . . . . . . . . .

8. . . . . . . . . . . . . . . . . . . . . . . . . . . . . . . . . . . . . . . . . . . . . . . . . . . . . . . . . .

Paul knew what many psychiatrists spend years studying: our thoughts become our actions. Paul didn't just want early Christians to act a better way—he wanted them to think a better way too. And it's still true today. We have to think a better way in order to act a better way.

### Live It!

How much better would your days be if your thoughts were only those eight things listed in Philippians 4:8?

. . . . . . . . . . . . . . . . . . . . . . . . . . . . . . . . . . . . . . . . . . . . . . . . . . . . . . . . . .
. . . . . . . . . . . . . . . . . . . . . . . . . . . . . . . . . . . . . . . . . . . . . . . . . . . . . . . . . .
. . . . . . . . . . . . . . . . . . . . . . . . . . . . . . . . . . . . . . . . . . . . . . . . . . . . . . . . . .

In what situations do you struggle the most with thinking good thoughts?

. . . . . . . . . . . . . . . . . . . . . . . . . . . . . . . . . . . . . . . . . . . . . . . . . . . . . . . . . .
. . . . . . . . . . . . . . . . . . . . . . . . . . . . . . . . . . . . . . . . . . . . . . . . . . . . . . . . . .
. . . . . . . . . . . . . . . . . . . . . . . . . . . . . . . . . . . . . . . . . . . . . . . . . . . . . . . . . .
. . . . . . . . . . . . . . . . . . . . . . . . . . . . . . . . . . . . . . . . . . . . . . . . . . . . . . . . . .

Make a commitment to walk away from anything that comes in front of you this week that isn't admirable, true, noble, or any of the other descriptions Paul gives us. There's an easy way to figure this out. Simply say, "Does this song, movie, joke, conversation, party, etc., bring glory to God's name?" If the answer is no, walk away.

## Ready, Set, Grow!

This week I will commit to

. . . . . . . . . . . . . . . . . . . . . . . . . . . . . . . . . . . . . . . . . . . . . . . . . . .

. . . . . . . . . . . . . . . . . . . . . . . . . . . . . . . . . . . . . . . . . . . . . . . . . . .

. . . . . . . . . . . . . . . . . . . . . . . . . . . . . . . . . . . . . . . . . . . . . . . . . . .

. . . . . . . . . . . . . . . . . . . . . . . . . . . . . . . . . . . . . . . . . . . . . . . . . . .

### Jealousy and Envy Are Just Wrong

ONE SUREFIRE WAY TO END or damage a relationship is through jealousy. Jealousy has a nickname, the "green-eyed monster." Maybe you've heard that term from your parents or, if you're a reader, from Shakespeare's play *Othello*. In the play, the character Iago says, "O, beware, my lord, of jealousy; It is the green-ey'd monster, which doth mock the meat it feeds on."

I did a little research and discovered that writers in Shakespeare's days liked to identify emotions with colors. Green and yellow were the colors for envy and jealousy. These two strong emotions are not exactly the same, but they are in the same family—I would say they're first cousins. While neither emotion can be totally avoided, we can learn to handle those emotions in a God-honoring way. First, let's look at the difference between envy and jealousy.

Envy is when you want something someone else has. Jealousy is when you think someone is trying to take something you have. For example, envy is obsessing over the car your best friend has, and jealousy is when you freak out because you think your best friend is trying to steal your boyfriend. Either way it's not good. When you think about it, jealousy and envy are emotions based on your own insecurity. Many believe that being jealous is a way of telling someone you really love and care about them. But that's just wrong. Loving someone is really about trusting them and giving them the freedom to grow and be who God wants them to be. Love is never about confinement. Jealousy confines a person to be who another person wants them to be. A jealous heart doesn't want the best for someone; it is only looking at what feels good. When you truly care about someone, you are happy for every victory they experience.

When I first started on *Dancing with the Stars*, it was hard for my boyfriend to watch me with my dance partner. I am so proud of how he searched his heart and was honest with me about the feelings he had. After praying and talking about it, he came to the right conclusion: my activities on the show were about me and the show and not about our relationship. I maintained a fun and healthy relationship with my partner on the show, and I learned an important lesson about love. My boyfriend loved me enough to let me go through that experience without hindering me. I am so thankful for his maturity and trust.

**Proverbs 14:30 (NLT)**

*A peaceful heart leads to a healthy body; jealousy is like cancer in the bones.*

⟫⟫⟫⟫ ——— Dig a Little Deeper ——— ⟪⟪⟪⟪

Jealousy is a serious emotion and not one to be played with. This verse refers to it as a cancer. We've gone through cancer in my family, and I'm sure some of you have too. It is a terrible disease that eats away at what was once healthy tissue. Jealousy does the same. It can eat away at a healthy relationship and destroy it.

Read James 3:16 (NIV) and fill in the blanks.

*For where you have .............. and .............. ambition, there you find .............. and every .............. practice.*

Read Philippians 2:3–4 (NIV).

*Do nothing out of .............. ambition or vain conceit. Rather, in .............. value .............. above yourselves, not looking to your own interests but each of you to the .............. of the .............. .*

Read Proverbs 14:30 (NLT) again, and fill in the blanks:

A .............. *heart leads to a* .............. *body;* ............. *is*
*like* .............. *in the bones.*

Maybe you can relate to the example I gave earlier about my boyfriend, and you have had to work through similar issues of jealousy in your own relationships. But jealousy isn't just found in boy-girl relationships. We all know that jealousy and its evil cousin, envy, can damage many girlfriend relationships. It's easy to feel envious of someone, especially when we start to think someone is more fortunate than we are. This can be concerning our looks, our talents, the position we hold in our school group, and anything else we think is important. Social media hasn't helped us out either, has it? It's crazy to see the many posts about beach trips, pedicures, new shoes, BFFs, and a gazillion other great things other people seem to have. It can cause us to question everything we have. Then that green-eyed monster, jealousy, can attack us when we think someone might be getting too close to that new girl at school.

So how do we walk away from jealousy and envy? First, when you feel envy or jealousy, stop and take a breath. Then it's time for some serious self-talk. Talk to yourself about the relationship in question and be honest about the feelings you are having. Here are some good questions to ask yourself.

What are you envious or jealous about?

. . . . . . . . . . . . . . . . . . . . . . . . . . . . . . . . . . . . . . . . . . . . . . . . . . . . . . . . . . .

. . . . . . . . . . . . . . . . . . . . . . . . . . . . . . . . . . . . . . . . . . . . . . . . . . . . . . . . . . .

. . . . . . . . . . . . . . . . . . . . . . . . . . . . . . . . . . . . . . . . . . . . . . . . . . . . . . . . . . .

. . . . . . . . . . . . . . . . . . . . . . . . . . . . . . . . . . . . . . . . . . . . . . . . . . . . . . . . . . .

Look a little deeper in your heart. What are you afraid will happen?

. . . . . . . . . . . . . . . . . . . . . . . . . . . . . . . . . . . . . . . . . . . . . . . . . . . . . . . . . . .

. . . . . . . . . . . . . . . . . . . . . . . . . . . . . . . . . . . . . . . . . . . . . . . . . . . . . . . . . . .

. . . . . . . . . . . . . . . . . . . . . . . . . . . . . . . . . . . . . . . . . . . . . . . . . . . . . . . . . . .

. . . . . . . . . . . . . . . . . . . . . . . . . . . . . . . . . . . . . . . . . . . . . . . . . . . . . . . . . . .

If you are envious of something someone else has or is doing, are you capable of having that or doing that particular thing?

. . . . . . . . . . . . . . . . . . . . . . . . . . . . . . . . . . . . . . . . . . . . . . . . . . . . . . . . . . .

. . . . . . . . . . . . . . . . . . . . . . . . . . . . . . . . . . . . . . . . . . . . . . . . . . . . . . . . . . .

. . . . . . . . . . . . . . . . . . . . . . . . . . . . . . . . . . . . . . . . . . . . . . . . . . . . . . . . . . .

. . . . . . . . . . . . . . . . . . . . . . . . . . . . . . . . . . . . . . . . . . . . . . . . . . . . . . . . . . .

List some things you can do or are doing that are uniquely you.

. . . . . . . . . . . . . . . . . . . . . . . . . . . . . . . . . . . . . . . . . . . . . . . . . . . . . . . . . . .

. . . . . . . . . . . . . . . . . . . . . . . . . . . . . . . . . . . . . . . . . . . . . . . . . . . . . . . . . . .

. . . . . . . . . . . . . . . . . . . . . . . . . . . . . . . . . . . . . . . . . . . . . . . . . . . . . . . . . . .

. . . . . . . . . . . . . . . . . . . . . . . . . . . . . . . . . . . . . . . . . . . . . . . . . . . . . . . . . . .

If you are jealous that someone might take a friendship away from you, list some ways you could include everyone involved to make sure everyone has friendship.

. . . . . . . . . . . . . . . . . . . . . . . . . . . . . . . . . . . . . . . . . . . . . . . . . . . . .

. . . . . . . . . . . . . . . . . . . . . . . . . . . . . . . . . . . . . . . . . . . . . . . . . . . . .

. . . . . . . . . . . . . . . . . . . . . . . . . . . . . . . . . . . . . . . . . . . . . . . . . . . . .

. . . . . . . . . . . . . . . . . . . . . . . . . . . . . . . . . . . . . . . . . . . . . . . . . . . . .

## ⪼ Ready, Set, Grow! ⪻

This week I will not let envy or jealousy enter my life. I will stop it by

. . . . . . . . . . . . . . . . . . . . . . . . . . . . . . . . . . . . . . . . . . . . . . . . . . . . .

. . . . . . . . . . . . . . . . . . . . . . . . . . . . . . . . . . . . . . . . . . . . . . . . . . . . .

. . . . . . . . . . . . . . . . . . . . . . . . . . . . . . . . . . . . . . . . . . . . . . . . . . . . .

. . . . . . . . . . . . . . . . . . . . . . . . . . . . . . . . . . . . . . . . . . . . . . . . . . . . .

## Just Do It

"JUST DO IT" is Nike's trademark saying. While it challenges me to work hard in any sport, it's also a great life motto. We're in a time where people spend hours not really doing anything. "Just Do It" is a reminder to make a difference in the world instead of making excuses. Have you ever looked around and noticed how many of your friends are sitting in front of a screen of some kind all throughout the day? Whether it's texting someone on their phone or vegging out with a show on Netflix or picture-stalking a new kid at school, everyone is looking down. Now, I love my phone just like you do, but we've got to stop looking down and start looking up and, basically, just do something!

For seven years now, I have been blessed to go to the Dominican Republic to work in an orphanage. Some of the children in the orphanage have parents who can't afford to care for them, but others have no family at all. However, now we are considered their family. We send these children messages of love on Facebook, we mail gifts to them at Christmas, and we visit them every summer. Imagine if we told them we loved them, but we never did anything to show them that love. Would they know we love them? You see, "love" is an action word. We think of love as a feeling and something we really can't define, but true love is shown in our actions. That means we have to look up and get moving if we want to show others that we have love in our hearts.

I recently read a book by Megan Boudreaux. At twenty-four years old, Megan quit her job, sold everything she owned, and moved to Haiti. Her book is titled *Miracle on Voodoo Mountain*. It's an unbelievable story of faith, hope, and love. Megan has gone on to adopt four Haitian children and continues her work in Haiti with her husband. Her story is so inspiring because she didn't just talk about doing something; she did it. She set out in 2010 to save children who are being used as slaves and to give them a better life. She continues to do this today.

⁀⸜°⸝⸆ What Does the Bible Say about It? ⸌°⸜⸍⸜

**Matthew 5:14–15 (NIV)**
*You are the light of the world. A town built on a hill cannot be hidden. Neither do people light a lamp and put it under a bowl. Instead they put it on its stand, and it gives light to everyone in the house.*

This verse, Matthew 5:14, is the perfect verse when I think about the life of Megan Boudreaux and her work in Haiti. First of all, she really did take over a hill for God. It was an area that formerly had been used for voodoo magic by the local witch doctors. Megan redeemed that land for God's glory, and it now shines brightly in a country that has very few bright lights. Not only is the hill an actual light shining in the darkness of Haiti, but so is Megan. She didn't hide her light; she *did something* to let her light shine. This verse says YOU are the light of the world. That's you and me. That's people who claim Jesus Christ as their Lord and Savior.

This verse follows Matthew 5:3–12, which are commonly called the Beatitudes. These words of Jesus describe His true disciples. See if you can find the eight traits listed in the Beatitudes.

1. . . . . . . . . . . . . . . . . . . . . . . . . . . . . . . . . . . . . . . . . . . .

2. . . . . . . . . . . . . . . . . . . . . . . . . . . . . . . . . . . . . . . . . . . .

3. . . . . . . . . . . . . . . . . . . . . . . . . . . . . . . . . . . . . . . . . . . .

4. . . . . . . . . . . . . . . . . . . . . . . . . . . . . . . . . . . . . . . . . . . .

5. . . . . . . . . . . . . . . . . . . . . . . . . . . . . . . . . . . . . . . . . . . .

6. . . . . . . . . . . . . . . . . . . . . . . . . . . . . . . . . . . . . . . . . . . .

7. . . . . . . . . . . . . . . . . . . . . . . . . . . . . . . . . . . . . . . . . . . .

8. . . . . . . . . . . . . . . . . . . . . . . . . . . . . . . . . . . . . . . . . . . .

At our small Christian school, we make a big statement with our sports programs. Back in 1987, the football coaches first challenged their team to *not just talk the talk, but to walk the walk*. Our sports teams have used that motto ever since. It's another great life motto, like "Just Do It." If you want to make a difference in the world, you have to do more than talk. You must let your feet take you places you never dreamed you'd go, and let your hands do things you never dreamed they could do. If you have any interest in serving in another country, start by getting your passport and then tell God you are ready to *Just Do It!*

Whatever you feel called to do, close to home or far away, take the steps to do something and see what God does through you and in you.

## Ready, Set, Grow!

This week I will make steps toward going where God sends me or doing what he wants me to do by

. . . . . . . . . . . . . . . . . . . . . . . . . . . . . . . . . . . . . . . . . . . . . . . . .

. . . . . . . . . . . . . . . . . . . . . . . . . . . . . . . . . . . . . . . . . . . . . . . . .

. . . . . . . . . . . . . . . . . . . . . . . . . . . . . . . . . . . . . . . . . . . . . . . . .

. . . . . . . . . . . . . . . . . . . . . . . . . . . . . . . . . . . . . . . . . . . . . . . . .

## Kindness Is the Cornerstone

I TALKED ABOUT acts of random kindness in an earlier chapter, but there's more to kindness than randomly doing nice things. Kindness is treating those around you with respect. It's smiling and making others feel important. It's using words that bring others up instead of down. Kindness is something you can do every day, no matter where you are.

When I was young, my mom could hardly get me to smile. My Two-Mama says it was a good thing that I was a pretty pouter because I pouted in most pictures. I admit, I was a late smiler. But at some point, I discovered the power of a smile to make others feel good about life.

I recently read an article about Jane Fonda. If you don't know who she is, google her. She is a famous movie star who has been married several times. She isn't married now, but in an interview she was asked about her latest boyfriend. Her words were, "One of the things you should look for when you're looking for a partner should be kindness. They don't teach you that when you're young. They should."

It's sad to think no one taught Jane Fonda that kindness is

the cornerstone of any relationship. I'm so blessed that I've been raised in a family where kindness matters. Two words I hear most often from my mom are "Be kind." In fact, my mom feels so passionate about it she titled her book *Strong and Kind*.

We have many people around our house. Our cousins live on the same street as us, so every day kids are in and out of our house. Kids can be mean. My cousins aren't perfect and neither am I. We've had times when someone has said something unkind. That's when our parents step in and everyone gets a lecture on being kind. I'm so thankful for that. Kindness is a way of life, and it's the secret to a successful relationship.

## What Does the Bible Say about It?

**Ephesians 4:32 (NIV)**
*Be kind and compassionate to one another, forgiving each other, just as in Christ God forgave you.*

## Dig a Little Deeper

I love this verse. It really tells us three ways we should treat others. List those three things.

1. ...............................................................
2. ...............................................................
3. ...............................................................

Then it gives us the reason for this behavior. Fill in these blanks for Ephesians 4:32 (NIV).

*Just as in* ..................., *God* ................... *you.*

Read Ephesians 1:1. Who wrote Ephesians, and who did he write it to?

..............................................................................
..............................................................................
..............................................................................

Read Ephesians 1:16. What did Paul say that lets you know he loved the people at Ephesus?

..............................................................................
..............................................................................
..............................................................................

Read Ephesians 4:1. What did Paul hope the believers at Ephesus would get from his message?

..............................................................................
..............................................................................
..............................................................................

꩜꩜꩜ Live It! ꩜꩜꩜

While kindness often comes out of a love we have for someone, being kind is not dependent on loving another person. Being kind is dependent on loving God and making the decision that kindness will bring *Him* glory, not you glory. But once you have decided to treat others with kindness, you will probably find out that you feel better yourself. This is also because of God's design. God never asks us to do things that will not be good for us. God knows that being kind to others will benefit both parties. Make a pledge to yourself to be kind to everyone you meet this week. That means your siblings (I know, this might be hard, but you can do it), the kids at school, the driver who cuts you off—seriously, it means everyone. Try it for one week and I think you'll decide it's the best way to live!

### 🌱 Ready, Set, Grow! 🌿

This week I will be kind to

.............................................................

.............................................................

.............................................................

.............................................................

## Keep the First Things First

PRIORITIES. We hear adults talk about keeping our priorities straight all the time. It's usually in reference to a bad grade or when our rooms are a total mess. But what does that word really mean?

I think priorities are the things that are most valuable or most important to us. And, I have to tell you, often what American teens show the world we hold valuable is pretty messed up. Just a quick look through Instagram and you see that our priorities are often the beach, double and triple ear piercings, our BFFs, cool selfies, and, of course, fashion.

There's this C. S. Lewis quote that really makes me think. It's from a letter written in 1951 to Dom Bede Griffiths, a monk living in South India. C. S. Lewis said, "Put first things first and we get second things thrown in: put second things first and we lose both first and second things. We never get, say, even the sensual pleasure of food at its best when we are being greedy." I know, it's a lot to think about. Both C. S. Lewis and Dom Griffiths were deep thinkers—way out of my league! But what he was saying is simply this: You can't get "second" things by putting them first. Put important things first, and second things will come. That sounds like a good "Keep the First Things First" principle to help prioritize the important things in your life.

**Colossians 3:1–2 (NIV)**
*Since, then, you have been raised with Christ, set your hearts on things above, where Christ is, seated at the right hand of God. Set your minds on things above, not on earthly things.*

Dig a Little Deeper

Colossians 3:1–2 are great verses telling us where our priorities should be. Read the verse again and fill in the blanks to help the message stick in your heart.

*Since, then, ............... have been raised with ..............., set your hearts on things ..............., where Christ is, seated at the right hand of ............... . Set your ............... on things above, not on ............... things.*

What does it mean to you to "set your heart on things above"?

.................................................................
.................................................................
.................................................................
.................................................................

If you were living at the time of Paul (the apostle who wrote Colossians), what challenges do you think you would have faced?

. . . . . . . . . . . . . . . . . . . . . . . . . . . . . . . . . . . . . . . . . . . . . . . . . . . . .

. . . . . . . . . . . . . . . . . . . . . . . . . . . . . . . . . . . . . . . . . . . . . . . . . . . . .

. . . . . . . . . . . . . . . . . . . . . . . . . . . . . . . . . . . . . . . . . . . . . . . . . . . . .

Read Colossians 3:5–10. Do you think the people in Paul's day faced the same challenges we do today?

. . . . . . . . . . . . . . . . . . . . . . . . . . . . . . . . . . . . . . . . . . . . . . . . . . . . .

. . . . . . . . . . . . . . . . . . . . . . . . . . . . . . . . . . . . . . . . . . . . . . . . . . . . .

. . . . . . . . . . . . . . . . . . . . . . . . . . . . . . . . . . . . . . . . . . . . . . . . . . . . .

Name some of those challenges.

. . . . . . . . . . . . . . . . . . . . . . . . . . . . . . . . . . . . . . . . . . . . . . . . . . . . .

. . . . . . . . . . . . . . . . . . . . . . . . . . . . . . . . . . . . . . . . . . . . . . . . . . . . .

. . . . . . . . . . . . . . . . . . . . . . . . . . . . . . . . . . . . . . . . . . . . . . . . . . . . .

*Live It!*

When we truly believe that Jesus is our Lord and Savior, it makes it easier to put the first things first. Many people believe teens are selfish. That's a sad thought, isn't it? People who are selfish believe that the first or most important thing in life is THEM. When I was a little girl, I learned the JOY principle. The JOY principle is "Jesus first, Others second, You last." Maybe you learned it too. If not, it's never too late to learn and to put into practice this Godly principle. Knowing the JOY principle has helped me make the right choice on many occasions. When the first person we think about in any situation is Jesus, it's easier to do the right thing. In fact, many activities will be totally taken off the table and you won't even have to continue thinking about them. When I was on *Dancing with the Stars*, everyone wanted to know if my daddy had to approve every costume I wore. The truth is, it was more important for that choice to be mine because of my love for Jesus. I never want to wear anything that would bring shame to God. But my daddy would come under the "others" part of JOY. So I do want to consider what my dad wants for me as well. If I put Jesus first and then consider others in all my decisions, then the "you" part of it becomes easier. Write "JOY" on a small piece of paper and put that paper in your purse or by your phone so you will always remember who's number one in your life.

### Ready, Set, Grow!

This week I will show others who is number one in my life by

. . . . . . . . . . . . . . . . . . . . . . . . . . . . . . . . . . . . . . . . . . . . . . . . .

. . . . . . . . . . . . . . . . . . . . . . . . . . . . . . . . . . . . . . . . . . . . . . . . .

. . . . . . . . . . . . . . . . . . . . . . . . . . . . . . . . . . . . . . . . . . . . . . . . .

. . . . . . . . . . . . . . . . . . . . . . . . . . . . . . . . . . . . . . . . . . . . . . . . .

## Line Leaders Are Still Cool

WHEN I WAS IN ELEMENTARY SCHOOL, door holder and line leader were two of the most awesome jobs. At our school, the teachers had a chart that showed when our turn would come up. Usually that chart went in alphabetical order. With the last name of Robertson, I didn't get my turn until far into the school year. I had plenty of time to watch others successfully or unsuccessfully accomplish the task of holding a door or leading their classmates to choir or PE or the bathroom.

When my turn came, I was ready! I could walk down the hall at an even pace. I was great at keeping my arms to myself. I knew how to get to any place in the school, and most important, I didn't talk. Being the leader was a huge deal to me.

As I get older, I realize people still need a line leader. In my book *Live Original*, I tell the story of a friend who said he wished the kids at his school were more spiritual. I challenged him by saying, "What are you going to do about it?" As teenagers, we don't always think we can make a difference, but there are hundreds of teens every year who are leading by example. They are teens who are not afraid to stand up and lead the line of their peers to church, to a Christian camp, to a Christian concert, in a devotional—or even to lead them away from doing something harmful to their lives or hearts. We can be the ones to lead our friends along the right path.

Have you ever heard the saying "If you don't know where you're going, you'll probably end up somewhere else"? This means that even if we don't know where we're going, we will end up somewhere—and often not a good place. We might allow someone else to dictate our path. So first of all, know the right path. Once you do, you'll see many others who don't know where they're going. It's up to you to lead them. Be the line leader that your friends need today.

 What Does the Bible Say about It?

**Proverbs 14:12 (NIV)**
*There is a way that appears to be right, but in the end it leads to death.*

>>>>>———— Dig a Little Deeper ————<<<<<

Good line leaders are so important. I've seen kids follow other kids down destructive paths, even paths that looked okay or even normal for a teenager to follow. This verse warns us that some paths will appear okay, but they are not. That's why we have to stay alert and close to God.

Read Proverbs 1:7. Where does our knowledge begin?

. . . . . . . . . . . . . . . . . . . . . . . . . . . . . . . . . . . . . . . . . . . . . . . . . . .

. . . . . . . . . . . . . . . . . . . . . . . . . . . . . . . . . . . . . . . . . . . . . . . . . . .

. . . . . . . . . . . . . . . . . . . . . . . . . . . . . . . . . . . . . . . . . . . . . . . . . . .

What are your thoughts on fearing the Lord?

. . . . . . . . . . . . . . . . . . . . . . . . . . . . . . . . . . . . . . . . . . . . . . . . . . .

. . . . . . . . . . . . . . . . . . . . . . . . . . . . . . . . . . . . . . . . . . . . . . . . . . .

. . . . . . . . . . . . . . . . . . . . . . . . . . . . . . . . . . . . . . . . . . . . . . . . . . .

Is there such a thing as a healthy fear?

. . . . . . . . . . . . . . . . . . . . . . . . . . . . . . . . . . . . . . . . . . . . . . . . . . .

. . . . . . . . . . . . . . . . . . . . . . . . . . . . . . . . . . . . . . . . . . . . . . . . . . .

. . . . . . . . . . . . . . . . . . . . . . . . . . . . . . . . . . . . . . . . . . . . . . . . . . .

Read Psalm 25:14. What does God do for those who fear Him?

. . . . . . . . . . . . . . . . . . . . . . . . . . . . . . . . . . . . . . . . . . . . . . . . . . .

. . . . . . . . . . . . . . . . . . . . . . . . . . . . . . . . . . . . . . . . . . . . . . . . . . .

. . . . . . . . . . . . . . . . . . . . . . . . . . . . . . . . . . . . . . . . . . . . . . . . . . .

## Live It!

Having a healthy fear of someone is to be respectful of them and their position. The teachers I respect took charge of their classrooms and helped us lead and learn. Having a healthy fear of God would mean we would live each day respecting that He is the Lord of our lives. We can learn a lot about being a leader by watching others lead well and by paying attention to how God leads us.

Not only can we learn by watching, but we can learn by reading too. Did you know the book of Proverbs is full of short instructions for living an effective life on earth? And the cool thing is there are thirty-one chapters, one for every day of the month. You might want to read whichever one corresponds with the day of the month it is. It doesn't matter when you start. For instance, if it's May 6, read Proverbs 6. This is a great way to start reading the Bible every day.

## Ready, Set, Grow!

This week I will lead by example and

. . . . . . . . . . . . . . . . . . . . . . . . . . . . . . . . . . . . . . . . . . . . . . . . . . . . . . . . . .

. . . . . . . . . . . . . . . . . . . . . . . . . . . . . . . . . . . . . . . . . . . . . . . . . . . . . . . . . .

. . . . . . . . . . . . . . . . . . . . . . . . . . . . . . . . . . . . . . . . . . . . . . . . . . . . . . . . . .

. . . . . . . . . . . . . . . . . . . . . . . . . . . . . . . . . . . . . . . . . . . . . . . . . . . . . . . . . .

## Little by Little

THERE ARE FEW PLACES as special to me as the beach. And it's special for more reasons than you might guess.

Our family goes to the beach every summer, and it's one of the best weeks of our year. Usually we only go one time during the summer, so we savor every minute. One year I went on three different trips to the beach, and that was the best!

The beach isn't just about having fun, playing in the waves, and making sand castles; it's also a perfect place to connect with God. I can sit right by the water's edge, and the wonders of God seem to jump out at me. I see God's power and strength on the days when the waves crash up to the shore. When the ocean is still and silent, I feel God's calming presence. Some days we wake to dark clouds and a storm rolling in across the water. Then the next day we might wake up to a bright shining sun. On any of these mornings, I'm reminded that God is always with me, even on my toughest days.

But there's one little part of the beach that totally fascinates me. I say "little" because it's actually the very smallest part of the beach. Can you guess what I'm talking about? It's the sand. Have you ever picked up a grain of sand? It's hard to get just one tiny grain. Yet one grain by one grain, little by little, sand becomes a beautiful landscape for a beach. Sand, as tiny as it is and as beautiful as it becomes, can also be annoying. In fact, I know of some people who won't go to the beach because they can't stand sand in their hair, shoes, car, and other crazy places.

When someone asks me what it will take to change the world, I think about those tiny grains of sand. To me, changing the world means each of us doing our part, little by little, one step at a time. Change can be dramatic, like what a powerful sandstorm can do to an area, but usually change happens gradually like the formation of a sandy beach. Geologists say sand is basically what you get when rocks are broken down by weathering over hundreds of thousands of years. It's a long, steady process.

When you think you can't make a difference, think about that one grain of sand. Sometimes after we get home from a beach trip, I put on a shoe or grab a blanket and find one grain of sand still in it. That grain of sand requires me to do something because, as small as it is, it makes an impact.

You might be acting alone, but your actions will move someone else to take action. Think of that next time you sit on the beach or feel sand in your shoes. With each of us doing our part, we will change the world!

**Ephesians 2:10 (NIV)**
*For we are God's handiwork, created in Christ Jesus to do good works, which God prepared in advance for us to do.*

⇝⇝⇝ —— Dig a Little Deeper —— ⇜⇜⇜

According to Ephesians 2:10, we are God's handiwork. Exactly like each tiny grain of sand, we are made by God—and not only that, we are created for a purpose.

Can you find that purpose in the verse above?

. . . . . . . . . . . . . . . . . . . . . . . . . . . . . . . . . . . . . . . . . . . . . . . . . . . . . . . . . . . . . . . . .

. . . . . . . . . . . . . . . . . . . . . . . . . . . . . . . . . . . . . . . . . . . . . . . . . . . . . . . . . . . . . . . . .

. . . . . . . . . . . . . . . . . . . . . . . . . . . . . . . . . . . . . . . . . . . . . . . . . . . . . . . . . . . . . . . . .

Think about it. From the time you were created, God planned for you to do good works. That's exactly what this verse tells us. Let's look at another Bible translation of this verse in *The Message*. This version was translated by a man named Eugene H. Peterson into a more contemporary style. His goal was to create a Bible that would be more easily understood. Look at how he translated the same verse and a few preceding it.

**Ephesians 2:7–10, *The Message* (MSG)**
*Now God has us where he wants us, with all the time in this*

*world and the next to shower grace and kindness upon us in Christ Jesus. Saving is all his idea, and all his work. All we do is trust him enough to let him do it. It's God's gift from start to finish! We don't play the major role. If we did, we'd probably go around bragging that we'd done the whole thing! No, we neither make nor save ourselves. God does both the making and saving. He creates each of us by Christ Jesus to join him in the work he does, the good work he has gotten ready for us to do, work we had better be doing.*

What does God shower on us?

........................ and ........................

What is His idea and all His work?

.............................................

.............................................

.............................................

What is our job?

.............................................

.............................................

.............................................

## Live It!

It's human nature to want to feel important and needed. You might be in a situation right now where you don't feel very important. You might not feel like you can make a difference.

But now is the time to trust God. You might be in a family of strong believers, all hard at work for God. You may not feel like you can contribute much. But you are wasting time comparing yourself to anyone else, even to your amazing grandfather who is a preacher. Don't compare—jump in there and do your part. You might be the only believer in your family. Great! Start showing everyone in your family what it means to know God. They will see the difference. You might lead them all to Him. Don't let anyone say you can't do something or that it's not going to work. If it's God's plan, it cannot be stopped. Above all else, pray that God will send you ideas that will change the world. You can do it, one step at a time.

## Ready, Set, Grow!

This week I will take a step to change the world by

. . . . . . . . . . . . . . . . . . . . . . . . . . . . . . . . . . . . . . . . . . . . . . . . . . .

. . . . . . . . . . . . . . . . . . . . . . . . . . . . . . . . . . . . . . . . . . . . . . . . . . .

. . . . . . . . . . . . . . . . . . . . . . . . . . . . . . . . . . . . . . . . . . . . . . . . . . .

. . . . . . . . . . . . . . . . . . . . . . . . . . . . . . . . . . . . . . . . . . . . . . . . . . .

*Love Your Selfie*

EVERY DAY ON SOCIAL MEDIA, most of the photos are selfies. "Selfie" wasn't even a word until a few years ago. Did you know "selfie" was named the Oxford Dictionaries Word of the Year for 2013? I didn't even know there was a word of the year! Along with "selfie" being a big player in our vocabulary, now we've added another term: "selfie stick." Some think the selfie stick is the best invention of 2015—even my grandma uses one! (This is actually better than her trying to take a selfie with one hand. She's pretty bad without her selfie stick.)

Even though the word "selfie" is new to this generation, the actual selfie is not. My grandma says cameras have had self-timers on them for years, and this is how they took pictures at family reunions. Modern technology has made it much easier. All you have to do is turn the camera on your phone around and push the button. (Seriously, Two-Mama, it's not that hard. Ha!)

But here is what is hard: understanding that taking a good picture of yourself, posting it, and counting likes and reading comments is not the way to gain a healthy self-esteem. Selfies are not designed to help you love the "you" God created you to be. Selfies are about bringing people *into* your world, but a healthy self-esteem comes from living *outside* of your world. Even better than self-esteem is self-respect. Self-respect makes us not need constant attention on social media.

How do we live outside of our world and have self-esteem and self-respect? We do this by viewing ourselves through God's eyes instead of our social media contacts, and by reaching to others, working hard, and making the right choices.

When our main focus of the day is getting the perfect "selfie," we are robbing ourselves of being the best we can be. I want my days to be about helping others and feeling confidence in who I am with God. I never feel as good about myself as I do when I am helping someone else and making God happy.

Let's commit to aiming for self-respect, and let's show God a selfie of us that will make him proud.

### What Does the Bible Say about It?

**Romans 12:3 (NIV)**
*For by the grace given me I say to every one of you: Do not think of yourself more highly than you ought, but rather think of yourself with sober judgment, in accordance with the faith God has distributed to each of you.*

You may not realize that the Bible has been translated by several different groups of really smart people. Just a few of those translations are the New International Version, the King James Version, the New Living Translation, *The Message*, and many more. If you are new to studying the Bible, this might seem shocking, but it's important to realize that the Bible was originally written in Hebrew and Greek. Just because there are different translations doesn't mean the words are not God-inspired. If someone, or lots of people, had not spent countless hours translating it for us, we would not have access to God's Word. As you study the Bible more and more, you will want to find a translation you like. Read these different translations of Romans 12:3. Don't forget to go back and read the version printed on the previous page.

**King James Version (KJV)**
*For I say, through the grace given unto me, to every man that is among you, not to think of himself more highly than he ought to think; but to think soberly, according as God hath dealt to every man the measure of faith.*

**New Living Translation (NLT)**
*Because of the privilege and authority God has given me, I give each of you this warning: Don't think you are better than you really are. Be honest in your evaluation of yourselves, measuring yourselves by the faith God has given us.*

### The Message (MSG)

*I'm speaking to you out of deep gratitude for all that God has given me, and especially as I have responsibilities in relation to you. Living then, as every one of you does, in pure grace, it's important that you not misinterpret yourselves as people who are bringing this goodness to God. No, God brings it all to you. The only accurate way to understand ourselves is by what God is and by what he does for us, not by what we are and what we do for him.*

What version do you like best?

. . . . . . . . . . . . . . . . . . . . . . . . . . . . . . . . . . . . . . . . . . . . . . . . . . . . . . . . .

. . . . . . . . . . . . . . . . . . . . . . . . . . . . . . . . . . . . . . . . . . . . . . . . . . . . . . . . .

. . . . . . . . . . . . . . . . . . . . . . . . . . . . . . . . . . . . . . . . . . . . . . . . . . . . . . . . .

Do the different versions give a different meaning?

. . . . . . . . . . . . . . . . . . . . . . . . . . . . . . . . . . . . . . . . . . . . . . . . . . . . . . . . .

. . . . . . . . . . . . . . . . . . . . . . . . . . . . . . . . . . . . . . . . . . . . . . . . . . . . . . . . .

. . . . . . . . . . . . . . . . . . . . . . . . . . . . . . . . . . . . . . . . . . . . . . . . . . . . . . . . .

What version of the Bible are you currently reading from?

. . . . . . . . . . . . . . . . . . . . . . . . . . . . . . . . . . . . . . . . . . . . . . . . . . . . . . . . .

. . . . . . . . . . . . . . . . . . . . . . . . . . . . . . . . . . . . . . . . . . . . . . . . . . . . . . . . .

. . . . . . . . . . . . . . . . . . . . . . . . . . . . . . . . . . . . . . . . . . . . . . . . . . . . . . . . .

This verse makes one very important point. Can you tell what it is?

. . . . . . . . . . . . . . . . . . . . . . . . . . . . . . . . . . . . . . . . . . . . . . . . . . . . . . . . .

. . . . . . . . . . . . . . . . . . . . . . . . . . . . . . . . . . . . . . . . . . . . . . . . . . . . . . . . .

I'm pretty sure you got it—the message is to not think more highly of yourself than you should. I heard this expression the other day: "You're exceptional, but you're not the exception." You might have to read that sentence twice to get it. In other words, in God's eyes we're the greatest thing since sliced bread (sorry, old expression borrowed from my grandparents), but we're not so unique that someone else hasn't done, experienced, lived, become, or tried anything we can think of doing, thinking, acting, or creating. God wants us to be proud of who we are and to be confident in the person God created us to be, but He doesn't want us to get the big head about it. Get it?

Ephesians 4:2 helps us understand this: "Be completely humble and gentle; be patient, bearing with one another in love." Other words for humble are "meek," "unassuming," "modest," and "respectful." Jesus was the ultimate example of this concept. He was the king of Heaven and earth, yet He never presented himself higher than anyone else. He was a servant first, and in His service to others, He became a king.

## Live It!

Selfies are part of modern life and they probably won't ever go away. I'm not saying they need to, but it is important to not make them more valuable than other aspects of life. There is a lot of discussion about having healthy self-esteem when the more important goal should be to have healthy self-respect. Esteem means to think highly of yourself. We just read in Romans 12:3 that we should not think too highly of ourselves, so I don't know why there is so much talk about having good self-esteem. I believe it is important to love the "you" God made you to be. I'm all about being original and true to who you are, but taking more selfies isn't the way to accomplish that. If you're struggling with your self-image, don't take another selfie. Instead try spending time with someone who needs you. Focusing outside of yourself is the best way to feel better about yourself. You can even use your social media if you want to share how you did that. Post a pic of yourself feeding the hungry or visiting a nursing home or mowing your neighbor's yard. All of those activities are about helping others, but trust me, you will be helped too.

## Ready, Set, Grow!

This week I will work on loving myself by

. . . . . . . . . . . . . . . . . . . . . . . . . . . . . . . . . . . . . . . . . . . . . . . . . . . . . . . . . . . . . .

. . . . . . . . . . . . . . . . . . . . . . . . . . . . . . . . . . . . . . . . . . . . . . . . . . . . . . . . . . . . . .

. . . . . . . . . . . . . . . . . . . . . . . . . . . . . . . . . . . . . . . . . . . . . . . . . . . . . . . . . . . . . .

. . . . . . . . . . . . . . . . . . . . . . . . . . . . . . . . . . . . . . . . . . . . . . . . . . . . . . . . . . . . . .

*Mission Possible*

WHILE DREAMING BIG IS IMPORTANT, dreaming is just one part of the plan. The other part is taking action. That's how you'll see your dream become a reality. This is where many people abandon their dreams because most big dreams seem like an impossible mission.

In the early 1970s (way before I was even thought about), my Papaw Phil dreamed of inventing a better duck call. Papaw Phil noticed that duck calls didn't really sound like ducks. He told my Mamaw Kay that he was going to invent the perfect duck call and make them a million dollars. Now, my mamaw loves my papaw, but she wasn't so sure about this dream coming true since they were living in a tiny house and eating whatever fish Papaw could catch for dinner.

But Papaw Phil did what other successful people do—he stopped talking and starting working. To make the impossible become possible you have to work. Your hands have to get dirty, and your feet have to go where they have never gone before. The people who knew Papaw in those years say he was never without a piece of wood to whittle on as he worked at perfecting his duck call. When his call was finished, Papaw had to boldly go and ask others to invest in his dream. None of it was easy, but because he didn't quit, our family is where we are today. I am so grateful that my papaw not only had a dream but also took action.

In the last few years, I've been so blessed to work with nonprofits (these are organizations that do good works and don't make a profit) all over the world. Every nonprofit begins with a dream, but then action turns that dream to reality. I've met a woman in Shreveport, Louisiana, who works helping women get out of sex trafficking. I've met a man in Nicaragua who spends his days helping children in Latin American countries who are hungry and in need of clothing and school supplies. I've met American men and women who sacrifice the comforts of living in the United States to help those less fortunate in Haiti. All over the world there are men and women making seemingly impossible dreams into realities.

If you have a dream, don't just dream about it. Get to work and make it come true.

## What Does the Bible Say about It?

**Colossians 3:23–24 (NIV)**
*Whatever you do, work at it with all your heart, as working for the Lord, not for human masters, since you know that you will receive an inheritance from the Lord as a reward. It is the Lord Christ you are serving.*

"Work" is a word most of us don't like to hear. When a parent says, "I've got a job for you," most of us want to run and hide. This verse in Colossians might help us see work in a different light. Read it carefully and answer the following questions.

How hard are we to work at something?

. . . . . . . . . . . . . . . . . . . . . . . . . . . . . . . . . . . . . . . . . . . . . . . .

. . . . . . . . . . . . . . . . . . . . . . . . . . . . . . . . . . . . . . . . . . . . . . . .

. . . . . . . . . . . . . . . . . . . . . . . . . . . . . . . . . . . . . . . . . . . . . . . .

Who are we really working for?

. . . . . . . . . . . . . . . . . . . . . . . . . . . . . . . . . . . . . . . . . . . . . . . .

. . . . . . . . . . . . . . . . . . . . . . . . . . . . . . . . . . . . . . . . . . . . . . . .

. . . . . . . . . . . . . . . . . . . . . . . . . . . . . . . . . . . . . . . . . . . . . . . .

What reward do you think the writer is talking about?

. . . . . . . . . . . . . . . . . . . . . . . . . . . . . . . . . . . . . . . . . . . . . . . .

. . . . . . . . . . . . . . . . . . . . . . . . . . . . . . . . . . . . . . . . . . . . . . . .

. . . . . . . . . . . . . . . . . . . . . . . . . . . . . . . . . . . . . . . . . . . . . . . .

Read Genesis 2:15. What purpose did Adam and Eve have in the garden?

. . . . . . . . . . . . . . . . . . . . . . . . . . . . . . . . . . . . . . . . . . . . . . . .

. . . . . . . . . . . . . . . . . . . . . . . . . . . . . . . . . . . . . . . . . . . . . . . .

. . . . . . . . . . . . . . . . . . . . . . . . . . . . . . . . . . . . . . . . . . . . . . . .

Read Genesis 3:23. After Adam and Eve were banned from the garden, what were they to do?

. . . . . . . . . . . . . . . . . . . . . . . . . . . . . . . . . . . . . . . . . . . . . . . . . . .

. . . . . . . . . . . . . . . . . . . . . . . . . . . . . . . . . . . . . . . . . . . . . . . . . . .

. . . . . . . . . . . . . . . . . . . . . . . . . . . . . . . . . . . . . . . . . . . . . . . . . . .

. . . . . . . . . . . . . . . . . . . . . . . . . . . . . . . . . . . . . . . . . . . . . . . . . . .

## Live It!

After reading these scriptures we can see that God designed us to work. We might roll our eyes when Mom calls us to load the dishwasher, but we can know that loading the dishwasher will make Mom and God happy. And that's a good thing. The work that is required to bring a dream to reality is more than just loading the dishwasher or making a bed, but doing those small jobs successfully will be training ground for harder jobs.

Many people out there are worried about our generation. Many don't think we can rise to the challenge and do the hard work required to bring our dreams to reality. So let's prove them wrong. It might require us to take a stand against a popular belief, or we might have to live uncomfortably in a foreign land. My dad says if something isn't working one way, get creative. It's not good enough to have a big dream. We have to commit to it and keep working, getting creative, until the mission is complete. We can do this!

What dreams do you have for the future?

. . . . . . . . . . . . . . . . . . . . . . . . . . . . . . . . . . . . . . . . . . . . . . . . . . . . . . . .

. . . . . . . . . . . . . . . . . . . . . . . . . . . . . . . . . . . . . . . . . . . . . . . . . . . . . . . .

. . . . . . . . . . . . . . . . . . . . . . . . . . . . . . . . . . . . . . . . . . . . . . . . . . . . . . . .

What steps can you take now to make those dreams come true?

. . . . . . . . . . . . . . . . . . . . . . . . . . . . . . . . . . . . . . . . . . . . . . . . . . . . . . . .

. . . . . . . . . . . . . . . . . . . . . . . . . . . . . . . . . . . . . . . . . . . . . . . . . . . . . . . .

. . . . . . . . . . . . . . . . . . . . . . . . . . . . . . . . . . . . . . . . . . . . . . . . . . . . . . . .

## ❧ Ready, Set, Grow! ❧

This week I will work to make my dreams come true by

. . . . . . . . . . . . . . . . . . . . . . . . . . . . . . . . . . . . . . . . . . . . . . . . . . . . . . . .

. . . . . . . . . . . . . . . . . . . . . . . . . . . . . . . . . . . . . . . . . . . . . . . . . . . . . . . .

. . . . . . . . . . . . . . . . . . . . . . . . . . . . . . . . . . . . . . . . . . . . . . . . . . . . . . . .

. . . . . . . . . . . . . . . . . . . . . . . . . . . . . . . . . . . . . . . . . . . . . . . . . . . . . . . .

## Make New Friends

IN MY BOOK *Live Original*, I write about two sisters who came to my school and how we became good friends. I was a freshman in high school when they changed schools and came to mine. While I have been to many different places and in many new settings, I've never experienced walking into a new school. I'm sure they were nervous about everything. They were likely thinking, *Will the teachers be nice? How is the food? Will the work be too hard?* But the biggest question was probably *Will I make friends?*

Today one of those sisters is my sister-in-law, Mary Kate. She married John Luke in June of 2015. Even though I went through most of my childhood not knowing Mary Kate and her sister, Kelly, now I can't imagine my life without them.

I share this story so you will keep your eyes and heart open to making new friends. Many of us teens get so attached to our old friends (the ones you met the first day of kindergarten) that we don't even want to look at the new girl in school. Often we impose a fear of losing our old friends onto each other, and this keeps us from opening up to someone new. Also jealousy, that green-eyed monster, keeps us from allowing our friends the opportunity to meet others. Don't get caught up in that trap. We will all feel jealousy or pride at times, but don't act on those feelings. In fact, just stop the feelings if you feel them creep in. That's a time to talk yourself out of a bad attitude.

I've never been in Girl Scouts, but my Two-Mama sings a Girl Scout song to me. It goes like this: "Make new friends, but keep the old. One is silver and the other gold." I love this message. Making new friends doesn't mean your old friends will have to go away. Each friendship is as valuable as silver and gold, just as the song says. You never know—that new girl at school might one day become your sister-in-law!

## What Does the Bible Say about It?

**Proverbs 12:26 (NIV)**
*The righteous choose their friends carefully, but the way of the wicked leads them astray.*

 Dig a Little Deeper

The Bible has a lot to say about friendship, particularly in the book of Proverbs. Remember, Proverbs is a book made up of short pieces of instruction for good living (and as I said in another chapter, they are broken into thirty-one chapters, so you can read one each day of the month). Read each of these Proverbs and answer the question.

Read Proverbs 12:26. How should we choose our friends?

. . . . . . . . . . . . . . . . . . . . . . . . . . . . . . . . . . . . . . . . . . . . . . . . . . . . . . .
. . . . . . . . . . . . . . . . . . . . . . . . . . . . . . . . . . . . . . . . . . . . . . . . . . . . . . .
. . . . . . . . . . . . . . . . . . . . . . . . . . . . . . . . . . . . . . . . . . . . . . . . . . . . . . .
. . . . . . . . . . . . . . . . . . . . . . . . . . . . . . . . . . . . . . . . . . . . . . . . . . . . . . .

Read Proverbs 16:28. What separates good friends?

. . . . . . . . . . . . . . . . . . . . . . . . . . . . . . . . . . . . . . . . . . . . . . . . . . . . . . .
. . . . . . . . . . . . . . . . . . . . . . . . . . . . . . . . . . . . . . . . . . . . . . . . . . . . . . .
. . . . . . . . . . . . . . . . . . . . . . . . . . . . . . . . . . . . . . . . . . . . . . . . . . . . . . .
. . . . . . . . . . . . . . . . . . . . . . . . . . . . . . . . . . . . . . . . . . . . . . . . . . . . . . .

Read Proverbs 18:24. What happens when we have unreliable
friends?

. . . . . . . . . . . . . . . . . . . . . . . . . . . . . . . . . . . . . . . . . . . . . . . . . . . . . . .
. . . . . . . . . . . . . . . . . . . . . . . . . . . . . . . . . . . . . . . . . . . . . . . . . . . . . . .
. . . . . . . . . . . . . . . . . . . . . . . . . . . . . . . . . . . . . . . . . . . . . . . . . . . . . . .
. . . . . . . . . . . . . . . . . . . . . . . . . . . . . . . . . . . . . . . . . . . . . . . . . . . . . . .

Read Proverbs 22:24. What kind of person should we avoid as
a friend?

. . . . . . . . . . . . . . . . . . . . . . . . . . . . . . . . . . . . . . . . . . . . . . . . . . . . . . .
. . . . . . . . . . . . . . . . . . . . . . . . . . . . . . . . . . . . . . . . . . . . . . . . . . . . . . .
. . . . . . . . . . . . . . . . . . . . . . . . . . . . . . . . . . . . . . . . . . . . . . . . . . . . . . .
. . . . . . . . . . . . . . . . . . . . . . . . . . . . . . . . . . . . . . . . . . . . . . . . . . . . . . .

Now that you've read the scriptures above, what kind of friend do you want to be?

. . . . . . . . . . . . . . . . . . . . . . . . . . . . . . . . . . . . . . . . . . . . .

. . . . . . . . . . . . . . . . . . . . . . . . . . . . . . . . . . . . . . . . . . . . .

. . . . . . . . . . . . . . . . . . . . . . . . . . . . . . . . . . . . . . . . . . . . .

. . . . . . . . . . . . . . . . . . . . . . . . . . . . . . . . . . . . . . . . . . . . .

List some of your old friends.

. . . . . . . . . . . . . . . . . . . . . . . . . . . . . . . . . . . . . . . . . . . . .

. . . . . . . . . . . . . . . . . . . . . . . . . . . . . . . . . . . . . . . . . . . . .

. . . . . . . . . . . . . . . . . . . . . . . . . . . . . . . . . . . . . . . . . . . . .

. . . . . . . . . . . . . . . . . . . . . . . . . . . . . . . . . . . . . . . . . . . . .

List some new friends.

. . . . . . . . . . . . . . . . . . . . . . . . . . . . . . . . . . . . . . . . . . . . .

. . . . . . . . . . . . . . . . . . . . . . . . . . . . . . . . . . . . . . . . . . . . .

. . . . . . . . . . . . . . . . . . . . . . . . . . . . . . . . . . . . . . . . . . . . .

. . . . . . . . . . . . . . . . . . . . . . . . . . . . . . . . . . . . . . . . . . . . .

If you don't have any new friends to list, get to work and find some. When you go to school this week or when you are out playing sports or whatever you do, meet someone new. I know, it's scary. But you can do it. Someone once said the hardest part of running is putting on your shoes. That means deciding to do it is the hard part. So decide you're going to make a new friend—and, like the verses said, choose your friends carefully. And then do it. You will make someone very happy this week, including yourself.

This week I will make one new friend by

. . . . . . . . . . . . . . . . . . . . . . . . . . . . . . . . . . . . . . . . . . . . . . . . . .

. . . . . . . . . . . . . . . . . . . . . . . . . . . . . . . . . . . . . . . . . . . . . . . . . .

. . . . . . . . . . . . . . . . . . . . . . . . . . . . . . . . . . . . . . . . . . . . . . . . . .

. . . . . . . . . . . . . . . . . . . . . . . . . . . . . . . . . . . . . . . . . . . . . . . . . .

THERE ARE SO MANY THINGS that have happened in my life since our TV show started in 2012. Things I never dreamed would happen. I try hard to learn from each experience I go through, and I hope you do the same with your experiences.

One life lesson I have learned through all of my activities is to never give up. My practices for *Dancing with the Stars* were very difficult. I had no dance experience, so I didn't even know how to count to the music (actually I never got that down), much less how to point my toes (still working on that one too). With no experience, I had to work extra hard for each new dance. Every week, when our new music and dance were assigned to us, I would think, *There's no way I can do that!* Have you ever thought that before? We all have. I've also looked at a math or an English assignment and thought the same thing. But I definitely learned through *Dancing with the Stars* that if you put your mind to something and never give up, you can do it.

Okay, I have a confession to make. My favorite TV show is

*Survivor*. My mom, Two-Mama, and I get together as much as we can to watch it. I love the competition and the spirit of "never give up" that it takes to survive in the wilderness. Another TV show I like is *Running Wild with Bear Grylls*. Again, it's another crazy survivor show. I read that Bear Grylls said, "Survival can be summed up in three words, 'Never give up.' That's the heart of it—really. Just keep trying."

I want to apply this same attitude to everything I do in life. Don't be guilty of giving up when you're just a few steps or days or practices away from going from good to great!

Whether you get to dance on *Dancing with the Stars* or on the stage at your local theater, or you're the point guard for your basketball team, or you help take care of your siblings while your mom works, you are learning valuable life lessons every day in everything you do. So in whatever you do, never give up!

### What Does the Bible Say about It?

**1 Samuel 17:45 (NIV)**

*David said to the Philistine, "You come against me with sword and spear and javelin, but I come against you in the name of the LORD Almighty, the God of the armies of Israel, whom you have defied."*

I hope you have heard the story of David and Goliath. Every time I read it, I learn something new. Recently I looked at the story with new eyes. Instead of thinking of David as the young, powerless shepherd boy, I thought of him as the wise and powerful leader that he truly was. We are often told in our Sunday school classes that David was a young boy who killed a giant with just a slingshot. We're also told he didn't want to wear the armor offered to him because he wasn't used to it. And we're told that no one believed he could slay the giant. All of that is true, but as I studied this seemingly simple story more, I realized three important things about David.

1. David knew his enemy. David looked at that giant, who was outfitted with a sword and javelin, and knew he could run faster without the heavy armor Saul offered him. To fight with his sword, Goliath would have to get close to David. David knew that wasn't going to happen. Read 1 Samuel 17:39. What did David say about the armor?

. . . . . . . . . . . . . . . . . . . . . . . . . . . . . . . . . . . . . . . . . . . . . . . .

. . . . . . . . . . . . . . . . . . . . . . . . . . . . . . . . . . . . . . . . . . . . . . . .

. . . . . . . . . . . . . . . . . . . . . . . . . . . . . . . . . . . . . . . . . . . . . . . .

2. David knew his ability. Read 1 Samuel 17:36. What had David done in his past that convinced him he could do this job?

. . . . . . . . . . . . . . . . . . . . . . . . . . . . . . . . . . . . . . . . . . . . . . . .

3. David knew his God. Read 1 Samuel 17:45. Who did David say was behind him?

David accurately viewed the situation. He knew what all the other warriors didn't know; he knew he could do it. Understanding what we are up against, what our talents are, and who is behind us will give us the same never-give-up attitude David had.

~~~~~~~~~ Live It! ~~~~~~~~~

What is something in your life that you have given up on?

Who are some of your real-life heroes who have never given up?

Do you see the same character traits in your heroes that David had?

. . . . . . . . . . . . . . . . . . . . . . . . . . . . . . . . . . . . . . . . . . . . . . . . . . . . . . . .

. . . . . . . . . . . . . . . . . . . . . . . . . . . . . . . . . . . . . . . . . . . . . . . . . . . . . . . .

. . . . . . . . . . . . . . . . . . . . . . . . . . . . . . . . . . . . . . . . . . . . . . . . . . . . . . . .

What are some other character traits needed to never give up?

. . . . . . . . . . . . . . . . . . . . . . . . . . . . . . . . . . . . . . . . . . . . . . . . . . . . . . . .

. . . . . . . . . . . . . . . . . . . . . . . . . . . . . . . . . . . . . . . . . . . . . . . . . . . . . . . .

. . . . . . . . . . . . . . . . . . . . . . . . . . . . . . . . . . . . . . . . . . . . . . . . . . . . . . . .

. . . . . . . . . . . . . . . . . . . . . . . . . . . . . . . . . . . . . . . . . . . . . . . . . . . . . . . .

## Ready, Set, Grow!

This week I will not give up on

. . . . . . . . . . . . . . . . . . . . . . . . . . . . . . . . . . . . . . . . . . . . . . . . . . . . . . . .

. . . . . . . . . . . . . . . . . . . . . . . . . . . . . . . . . . . . . . . . . . . . . . . . . . . . . . . .

. . . . . . . . . . . . . . . . . . . . . . . . . . . . . . . . . . . . . . . . . . . . . . . . . . . . . . . .

. . . . . . . . . . . . . . . . . . . . . . . . . . . . . . . . . . . . . . . . . . . . . . . . . . . . . . . .

## Obey (Yes, That's in the Bible)

SOMETIMES LITTLE KIDS WILL SAY, "You're not the boss of me." When I hear a kid say that, I cringe and think, *Oh no, this kid is going to have a problem with authority.*

In my book *Live Original*, I say there's a simple answer to the question "Who's the boss?" That answer is God.

Authority is just a way for our world to be organized. Think about a world with no one in charge. One time at our Christian camp, our directors thought it would be fun to play a no-rules basketball game. The result wasn't fun at all. Balls were flying, people got hurt, and everyone ended up mad at each other. It was out of control. That's how life would be if no one was in authority.

It's good for us to always remember God doesn't do anything that would be bad for us. Not anything! God knew without authority and obedience, the world would be like an out-of-control basketball game. God knows and sees the past, present, and future all at the same time. This is hard for us to comprehend because we see the world only in terms of what's happening right now. Teens struggle with obeying their parents because we can only see what we want to do in the current moment, and our parents see the bigger picture. God gave our parents authority over us for a reason. He knew we needed order that can come from someone older and wiser giving us a few rules. Think back to the out-of-control basketball game. Just a few rules and that game would have become fun again.

You and I are young now, but someday we will be in authority. My prayer is that I will always look to God and follow the example He gave me. I want to lead with love, patience, and kindness. I also want to be obedient to God, my parents, and others in authority in the same way.

## What Does the Bible Say about It?

**Ephesians 6:1–3 (NIV)**

*Children, obey your parents in the Lord, for this is right. "Honor your father and mother"—which is the first commandment with a promise—"so that it may go well with you and that you may enjoy long life on the earth."*

## Dig a Little Deeper

Read Ephesians 3:1 and 4:1. How does Paul describe himself?

. . . . . . . . . . . . . . . . . . . . . . . . . . . . . . . . . . . . . . . . . . . . . . . . . . .

. . . . . . . . . . . . . . . . . . . . . . . . . . . . . . . . . . . . . . . . . . . . . . . . . . .

. . . . . . . . . . . . . . . . . . . . . . . . . . . . . . . . . . . . . . . . . . . . . . . . . . .

. . . . . . . . . . . . . . . . . . . . . . . . . . . . . . . . . . . . . . . . . . . . . . . . . . .

Paul is a prisoner at the time of this writing. He was in prison because he was preaching about Jesus and that made the authorities mad. King Agrippa had listened to Paul's defense of his actions.

Read Acts 25:25 (NIV). Fill in the blanks.

*"I found he had done nothing deserving of* . . . . . . . . . . . . . . . . *, but because he made his appeal to the Emperor I decided to send him to* . . . . . . . . . . . . . . . . . . . . . . . . . *."*

Paul was sent to Rome. Read Acts 28:16. What were Paul's living conditions?

. . . . . . . . . . . . . . . . . . . . . . . . . . . . . . . . . . . . . . . . . . . . . . . . . . . . . . .
. . . . . . . . . . . . . . . . . . . . . . . . . . . . . . . . . . . . . . . . . . . . . . . . . . . . . . .
. . . . . . . . . . . . . . . . . . . . . . . . . . . . . . . . . . . . . . . . . . . . . . . . . . . . . . .
. . . . . . . . . . . . . . . . . . . . . . . . . . . . . . . . . . . . . . . . . . . . . . . . . . . . . . .

Paul, while being obedient to God, was also obedient to the authorities. He had to fulfill his prison sentence. He knew what the price would be for obedience and he also understood it was necessary.

Read Ephesians 6:1–3. Why did Paul say children should obey their parents?

. . . . . . . . . . . . . . . . . . . . . . . . . . . . . . . . . . . . . . . . . . . . . . . . . . . . . . .
. . . . . . . . . . . . . . . . . . . . . . . . . . . . . . . . . . . . . . . . . . . . . . . . . . . . . . .
. . . . . . . . . . . . . . . . . . . . . . . . . . . . . . . . . . . . . . . . . . . . . . . . . . . . . . .

What is the promise to children who are obedient?

As I said in an earlier lesson, knowing what we should do and actually doing it are two different things. Sometimes we know what we should do, but we don't always do it, right? Recently at the Christian school I go to, the principal had to make some new rules about the dress code because the girls' dresses kept getting shorter and shorter. The administration sent a letter around to the parents to see if they wanted to go to uniforms. What came back to the administration surprised them. The parents didn't want uniforms; they wanted the administration to enforce the rules they already had about the dress code. Here's the sad truth to all of that. If each girl would obey the rules, then the administration wouldn't have to enforce them. Think about it like this: laws are never made for the good guys; they're for the bad guys—the ones who don't do the right thing on their own. It's up to each one of us to be obedient. We are all called to obey and that obedience can be to our parents, our teachers, the laws of the land, or anyone else in authority. Learning to obey the people in authority on earth helps us to understand obedience to God. Determine today to be one of the good guys. Be the one the laws or rules aren't made for because you do the right thing anyway.

## ❧ Ready, Set, Grow! ❧

This week I will be obedient when I

. . . . . . . . . . . . . . . . . . . . . . . . . . . . . . . . . . . . . . . . . . . . .

. . . . . . . . . . . . . . . . . . . . . . . . . . . . . . . . . . . . . . . . . . . . .

. . . . . . . . . . . . . . . . . . . . . . . . . . . . . . . . . . . . . . . . . . . . .

. . . . . . . . . . . . . . . . . . . . . . . . . . . . . . . . . . . . . . . . . . . . .

## Pride Comes Before a Fall

WHEN YOU THINK of the word "pride," do you think it's a positive trait or a negative trait? I have pride in my school and in my work. My parents take pride in their children. I love that we live in a country most people are proud of. So what's the deal with pride? The kind of pride I just described is pride that comes from hard work, respect, and a love for something.

But there's another kind of pride I want us to look at this week. It's the kind of pride that boasts when there is nothing to boast about, and it causes people to be blinded to their own faults. Pride, like jealousy and envy, can destroy people's character, reputations, and relationships. Some other words for pride are "smugness," "conceit," and "arrogance." None of those are words I want someone to use when describing me. A prideful person seeks the attention of others and values being better than others. There's so much wrong with that! God is very clear that humility, goodness, and kindness are the traits He values.

The famous writer C. S. Lewis said, "A proud man is always looking down on things and people, and, of course, as long as you're looking down, you can't see something above you." I'm pretty sure he was saying if we're busy looking down at people, we won't look up to see God. How true is that? Looking up always demands a posture of humility. When I was little and wanted to be heard, I would stand on the fireplace. My goal was to get higher than everyone so they would have to look up at me. I'm happy to report I have learned my place in this world and it's not on top of the fireplace. It's at the feet of Jesus.

## What Does the Bible Say about It?

**Proverbs 16:18 (NIV)**
*Pride goes before destruction, a haughty spirit before a fall.*

## Dig a Little Deeper

The Bible has a lot to say about pride. God is not happy with the prideful person.

Read the following scriptures and fill in the blanks.

**Proverbs 8:13 (NIV)**
*To fear the Lord is to hate evil; I hate ..................... and ....................., evil behavior and perverse speech.*

**Proverbs 11:2 (NIV)**
*When ..................... comes, then comes ....................., but with humility comes ......................*

**Proverbs 14:3 (NIV)**

*A fool's mouth lashes out with* ...................... *, but the lips of the* ...................... *protect them.*

~~~~~~~~~~~~~~~~~~~~~~~ Live It! ~~~~~~~~~~~~~~~~~~~~~~~

Nobody wants to hang out with people who think they are better than others. Can you think of a reason someone would act prideful?

......................................................................

......................................................................

......................................................................

......................................................................

Since character traits are shown in our actions, pride is revealed in our attitudes and actions toward others. Some people might act prideful to cover up something going on in their life, like a breakup or bad grades. It's important for us to be open to every possibility and really listen to our friends. It's also possible for someone to appear prideful when they are really shy and don't know how to handle social situations.

If you have been guilty of being prideful, determine today to put it behind you. Next, if you have treated someone who is prideful unkindly, then you need to repent of that too. Remember, your goal is to be the best you can be, not to be better than everyone else.

## Ready, Set, Grow!

To make sure I do not have an attitude of pride, I will

....................................................

....................................................

....................................................

....................................................

## Quiet Time with God

A FEW YEARS AGO AT SUMMER CAMP, the directors decided it would be good for the campers to experience some quiet time. We were given what seemed like an eternity in the woods, completely by ourselves. I seriously thought I would go crazy. I wasn't used to quiet time. There's no quiet time in a house with six kids, two parents, and four dogs. Besides that, I'm not a quiet time kind of girl. If I have a few hours free, I quickly fill them up. If I am home alone for a few minutes, I walk next door to my grandma's. If my mom and I are the only ones in the house for the night, I ask to sleep with her. You get the picture.

I'm pretty sure many of you are a lot like me. We're busy teenagers with a lot going on. But since the quiet time challenge at summer camp, I've grown and matured. (At least, I think I have.) The following summer, I went to another camp that was held at the beach, and it was there I learned the power of quiet time. Perhaps it was the solitude of the beach or the beauty of it that got my attention. I just know I finally got it. Now I understand time alone with God isn't just about enduring a silent moment; it's about learning to talk with Him and listen to Him.

In some ways, our relationship with God is similar to any other relationship we have. None of our relationships will grow if we ignore them, but that is what we often do to God. We ignore Him, except when we really need Him. I don't want to be guilty of treating God like He's a holy vending machine.

Jesus knew the importance of quiet time. In Mark 1:35 it tells us Jesus got up very early in the morning to find a place to pray. Jesus set an example for us and, sadly, many of us don't follow that example.

I was honored to be a part of the Rachel Scott movie, *I'm Not Ashamed*. Rachel was killed in the school shooting at her high school in Littleton, Colorado. Rachel loved God and was devoted to spending time with God. The words and thoughts she recorded in several diaries are a testimony to the time she spent with God. I read one of those diaries, and it made an impact on my life, as it does for many others who read about her. I'm thankful to have Rachel Scott as a model of how to emulate Jesus' prayerful living.

 What Does the Bible Say about It?

**Luke 5:16 (NIV)**
*But Jesus often withdrew to lonely places and prayed.*

Many times we think God doesn't understand us, but that's not true. The Bible tells us Jesus was tempted in every way, just like man. Read Hebrews 4:15 (NIV) and fill in the blanks.

*For we do not have a high priest who is* ........................ *to empathize with our* ........................, *but we have one who has been* ........................ *in every way, just as we are—yet he did not* .........................

We also might think we have more going on than Jesus. After all, we have school, homework, extracurricular activities, youth group activities, and things to do with our families. We don't have time for quiet time.

Read Luke 5:15 (NIV) and fill in the blanks.

*Yet the* ........................ *about him spread all the more, so that* ........................ *of people came to hear him and to be* ........................ *of their sicknesses.*

Jesus was also a busy man. What was He at work doing?

....................................................................

....................................................................

Even in His busyness, Jesus found time for God. Put in your own words Luke 5:16.

....................................................................

## Live It!

Carving out some time to sit still and get to know Jesus can be challenging. Start slowly. Try setting your alarm clock five or ten minutes earlier than you normally wake up. Have your Bible, a pen or pencil, and a notebook handy. If you've never done anything like this before, a good place to start is with a book like James. It only has five chapters and is full of tips on how to live a Christian life.

Once you start opening your heart to hear God's Word, you'll never regret it. It was hard for me to sit still at camp that year during quiet time, but now that I understand the importance of my God-time, that is no longer a problem. The more time you spend with God, the happier you will be, and you will actually look forward to your quiet time. You might even enjoy getting up thirty minutes earlier. Imagine that!

## Ready, Set, Grow!

This week I will get started on the path to more consistent quiet times with God by

## Responsibility Ability

THE GOAL OF EVERY HUMAN BEING should be to become a responsible person.

I've heard that we shouldn't let *our* emergency become someone else's problem. For example, every time you leave something at home and can't go back for it, it becomes your mom's problem to get it for you. Or if you have a car and don't get the oil changed, it becomes your dad's problem to fix a messed-up car (okay, I did this for real). Or when you are the last one out the door on a school day, it becomes your siblings' problem too because they are late to school. Do you see how our emergencies always affect someone else?

In today's world, teens are often thought of and portrayed in media outlets as irresponsible, eye-rolling, self-obsessing, pizza-eating humans between the ages of thirteen and nineteen. A few years ago two teens set out to prove that teenagers don't have to live down to this current American definition. Twins Alex and Brett Harris wrote a book called *Do Hard Things* when they were eighteen years old. Alex and Brett didn't just talk about doing hard things; they *did* hard things.

At age seventeen, they were the youngest interns on record at the Alabama Supreme Court.

Our youth group studied the book, and I promise, if you read it, you will be challenged to change. The subtitle of their book is *A Teenage Rebellion against Low Expectations*. Don't you love that? If I am going to be rebellious about anything, I want to rebel against having low expectations for myself. In their book, the twins say the teen years are not a vacation from responsibility, but are training grounds for future leaders who dare to be responsible.

Doing hard things always involves accepting personal responsibility. Becoming the responsible person we all need to be requires growing and stretching, just like working for anything else we do in life. We all know our muscles get stronger when we work them, and it's the same for our responsibility muscle. The more we put responsible behavior on the top of our list, the better we will get at doing it.

## What Does the Bible Say about It?

**Luke 1:38 (NIV)**

*"I am the Lord's servant," Mary answered. "May your word to me be fulfilled."*

You might think this is an unusual verse for me to use for a chapter on responsibility, but I think it's perfect. To me, Mary, the mother of Jesus, is the perfect example of a teen accepting and doing a very hard thing. You might be wondering how I know Mary was a teenager. First, we read that Mary was engaged to be married. Read Matthew 1:18 (NIV) and fill in the blanks.

*This is how the .................... of Jesus the Messiah came about: His mother ................ was pledged to be married to ................, but before they came together, she was found to be pregnant through the Holy Spirit.*

From historical writings, we know Jewish women of this day were always engaged before age fourteen. So we can conclude that Mary was a young teen when God sent an angel to her.

Read Luke 1:30–31 (NIV) and fill in the blanks.

*But the angel said to her, "Do not be ................, Mary; you have found ............... with God. You will conceive and give ............... to a son, and you are to call him ...............:*

We can't even imagine how Mary, a young teenager, must have felt when she heard these words. Most of us are worried about the outfit we'll wear this weekend or whether or not we should speak to that cute guy at school. From Mary's words, we know she was concerned. Read Luke 1:29 (NIV) and fill in the blanks.

*Mary was greatly* .............. *at his words and* .............. *what kind of greeting this might be.*

Mary was human just like we are and was troubled at the responsibility given to her, but she accepted it. Read Luke 1:38 again. It's your verse for the week.

What did Mary say that tells you she accepted her responsibility?

. . . . . . . . . . . . . . . . . . . . . . . . . . . . . . . . . . . . . . . . . . . . . . . . . . . . . . . .

. . . . . . . . . . . . . . . . . . . . . . . . . . . . . . . . . . . . . . . . . . . . . . . . . . . . . . . .

. . . . . . . . . . . . . . . . . . . . . . . . . . . . . . . . . . . . . . . . . . . . . . . . . . . . . . . .

. . . . . . . . . . . . . . . . . . . . . . . . . . . . . . . . . . . . . . . . . . . . . . . . . . . . . . . .

## Live It!

The whole idea of living responsibly is not always a fun idea, but it is the path to take if we want to become mature adults. Wouldn't it be great if people between the ages of thirteen and nineteen in America were *not* thought of as gum-chewing, pizza-loving, eye-rolling, irresponsible teens? List some words you would like to see teens described as.

1. . . . . . . . . . . . . . . . . . . . . . . . . . . . . . . . . . . . . . . . . . . . . . . . . . . . . . . .

2. . . . . . . . . . . . . . . . . . . . . . . . . . . . . . . . . . . . . . . . . . . . . . . . . . . . . . . .

3. ......................................................................

4. ......................................................................

The truth is teens have more energy, more passion, and more time than any other age group. Now is the time for us to start acting like this statement is true.

What is the biggest struggle you have right now with being responsible?

......................................................................

......................................................................

......................................................................

### ❧ Ready, Set, Grow! ❧

This week I will work on being more responsible by

......................................................................

......................................................................

......................................................................

......................................................................

## Sacrifice Something

TEENS DON'T OFTEN THINK of the word "sacrifice" in a positive light. My guess is no one really does. My personal definition of sacrifice is giving up something of importance for a greater purpose.

One year our family was in Hawaii filming for *Duck Dynasty*, but my basketball play-offs were coming up. I had a tough decision to make. Should I stay in Hawaii with my family, or should I fly home early to play with the team? Tough call, right (and you know how much I love the beach)? I decided to fly home. I sacrificed a few vacation days and time with my family to fulfill the obligations I knew I had agreed to when I signed up to play basketball for my school.

Sacrifice has to come from a deeper place than where we usually make a decision. It has to come from a sense of responsibility, love, and maturity. I think I made the mature decision to play ball, and I did it because I felt responsible to my team and I loved my teammates.

For all of us, we want the thing we are sacrificing for to have meaning, but the most important thing to "get" about sacrifice is that it's the right thing to do even if the outcome you want isn't realized.

When I think about the ultimate sacrifice of Jesus' death on the cross, I understand Jesus died that horrible death without being sure if anyone would follow Him. In other words, He didn't just give up His life because of a known and perfect outcome. He gave His life on the chance we would one day follow Him.

When I was debating in my head about playing that playoff game, one of the factors was that we wouldn't be guaranteed a win. In fact, we didn't win. I still believe I did the right thing.

## What Does the Bible Say about It?

**Hebrews 13:16 (NIV)**
*And do not forget to do good and to share with others, for with such sacrifices God is pleased.*

## Dig a Little Deeper

Read the verse for the week. It says, "Do not ............... to do good." Isn't it cool how God knows us? He knows we will "forget" to do good and "forget" to share, so He sends this little warning to us—it's a reminder like a sticky note that tells you to not forget money for the class field trip. There's something else I get from this verse. God knows doing good deeds and sharing with others requires us to sacrifice something. The entire chapter of Hebrews 13 is God's sticky note of reminders to us. What else are we reminded of in the following verses?

**Hebrews 13:2:**

........................................................................
........................................................................
........................................................................
........................................................................

**Hebrews 13:3:**

........................................................................
........................................................................
........................................................................
........................................................................

**Hebrews 13:7:**

........................................................................
........................................................................
........................................................................
........................................................................

Write in your own words why we are reminded to do these things. Look at Hebrews 13:16 for the answer.

........................................................................
........................................................................
........................................................................
........................................................................

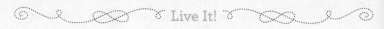 

Life is really a series of small sacrifices and, every now and then, a huge one. Think about it like this: When you go to bed at night, you have a decision to make as you set your alarm. You can either wake up early to eat a good breakfast, or you can sleep in and get a few extra minutes of much-needed sleep. With either decision, you are sacrificing something. We're actually very used to the concept of sacrificing little things. But what about some of the bigger things in life?

What was the last thing you sacrificed for?

. . . . . . . . . . . . . . . . . . . . . . . . . . . . . . . . . . . . . . . . . . . . . . . . . . . . . . . . .

. . . . . . . . . . . . . . . . . . . . . . . . . . . . . . . . . . . . . . . . . . . . . . . . . . . . . . . . .

. . . . . . . . . . . . . . . . . . . . . . . . . . . . . . . . . . . . . . . . . . . . . . . . . . . . . . . . .

. . . . . . . . . . . . . . . . . . . . . . . . . . . . . . . . . . . . . . . . . . . . . . . . . . . . . . . . .

Do you notice others around you making sacrifices? What are some of the sacrifices you see in others?

. . . . . . . . . . . . . . . . . . . . . . . . . . . . . . . . . . . . . . . . . . . . . . . . . . . . . . . . .

. . . . . . . . . . . . . . . . . . . . . . . . . . . . . . . . . . . . . . . . . . . . . . . . . . . . . . . . .

. . . . . . . . . . . . . . . . . . . . . . . . . . . . . . . . . . . . . . . . . . . . . . . . . . . . . . . . .

. . . . . . . . . . . . . . . . . . . . . . . . . . . . . . . . . . . . . . . . . . . . . . . . . . . . . . . . .

. . . . . . . . . . . . . . . . . . . . . . . . . . . . . . . . . . . . . . . . . . . . . . . . . . . . . . . . .

When you consider the bigger sacrifices in life, think about things we might need to sacrifice to live a faithful life to God. One of my uncles loved to play cards and was very good at it. But when he played, he noticed that he became rude and angry with others, so he quit playing. Playing cards interfered with him acting in a Christ-like way. Are there some things in your life that you love, but when you participate they cause you to act or think in an ungodly way? If there are, this week is the week to give them up.

## 🌱 Ready, Set, Grow! 🌿

This week I will sacrifice

. . . . . . . . . . . . . . . . . . . . . . . . . . . . . . . . . . . . . . . . . . . . . . . . . . .

. . . . . . . . . . . . . . . . . . . . . . . . . . . . . . . . . . . . . . . . . . . . . . . . . . .

. . . . . . . . . . . . . . . . . . . . . . . . . . . . . . . . . . . . . . . . . . . . . . . . . . .

. . . . . . . . . . . . . . . . . . . . . . . . . . . . . . . . . . . . . . . . . . . . . . . . . . .

## Say Something About Siblings

KNOW THAT'S A WEIRD CHAPTER TITLE, but I really want to say something about siblings, so there you have it. My family might be different from other families because I have three adopted siblings and two biological siblings. Sibling relationships can be the most difficult relationships we have on earth. There are many reasons for this. One is simple: we can't choose our siblings like we choose our friends. Another reason is that everyone has their own God-given personality and that can be very annoying when it's different from our own.

John Luke and I are very close now, but in our early teen years that wasn't the case. Our personalities are completely different. For example, when riding in an airplane, John Luke is relaxed and would love it if the pilot decided to do a few loops. However, I am praying the pilot got plenty of sleep, is not sick, drank plenty of coffee, and never goes through a cloud. John Luke is always looking for the adventure, but I'm looking for the emergency exit sign. If I were to describe all of my siblings, none of us are exactly the same. Some of us have more things in common than others, but mostly we are six different personalities.

While it's human nature for us to wish everyone was just like us, aren't we glad God had a different plan? I have a friend who uses the word "celebrate" when she talks about accepting the differences in others. She says we shouldn't just tolerate others; we should celebrate them. I have to say sometimes the sibling celebration is not happening. (Call me picky, but when I see a sibling chewing with their mouth open, it drives me crazy with a capital "C"!)

But sibling relationships are important to our maturity. They are our first look at community living. It's where we get to practice living with others who are different from us. How is your practice session going? Life is going to give us many areas to use our people skills, so your practice days are important. From college life to the work force, we will encounter many personality types and we will have to get along with them.

I've learned the most about celebrating people's differences from watching my mom. She loves each of her six children equally, even though we are all so different. She celebrates our differences and never expects one of us to do what the other does. She's taught us the most important thing to have in common is our love for Jesus Christ. If we've got that in place, everything else will work itself out.

**1 John 4:20 (NIV)**

*Whoever claims to love God yet hates a brother or sister is a liar. For whoever does not love their brother and sister, whom they have seen, cannot love God, whom they have not seen.*

Dig a Little Deeper

This is a powerful verse and one we shouldn't ignore. It's pretty bold to say anyone who claims to love God but hates a brother or sister is a liar, but God is serious about this. Remember, family is our first look at community life. God is serious about us getting along. The apostle John, who wrote this book, went on to say why claiming to love God while hating someone makes you a liar.

Is it easier to love someone we see and know?

. . . . . . . . . . . . . . . . . . . . . . . . . . . . . . . . . . . . . . . . . . . . .

. . . . . . . . . . . . . . . . . . . . . . . . . . . . . . . . . . . . . . . . . . . . .

. . . . . . . . . . . . . . . . . . . . . . . . . . . . . . . . . . . . . . . . . . . . .

. . . . . . . . . . . . . . . . . . . . . . . . . . . . . . . . . . . . . . . . . . . . .

Can you think of anyone you love but have never seen?

. . . . . . . . . . . . . . . . . . . . . . . . . . . . . . . . . . . . . . . . . . . . .

. . . . . . . . . . . . . . . . . . . . . . . . . . . . . . . . . . . . . . . . . . . . .

. . . . . . . . . . . . . . . . . . . . . . . . . . . . . . . . . . . . . . . . . . . . .

. . . . . . . . . . . . . . . . . . . . . . . . . . . . . . . . . . . . . . . . . . . . .

What causes us to not get along with our siblings? Read Galatians 5:26 (NIV).

*Let us not become conceited, provoking and envying each other.*

The three things listed in this verse are three root causes for relationship issues. List these three things.

1. ................................................................

2. ................................................................

3. ................................................................

## Live It!

We've all been guilty of thinking our brothers and sisters are aggravating and annoying. We rarely think our friends are that way. But guess what? Their brothers and sisters think they are just as annoying as you think your siblings are. The difference is you don't live with your friends. Living with someone requires more patience, love, and understanding. If you're not sure if living together changes a relationship, just ask best friends who decided to be roommates at college. I've heard of plenty who are no longer best friends after one semester of living together. The truth is, whether you're siblings, friends, or married people, your goal has to be the same thing: to learn to get along with others in a way that brings glory to God. Keep in mind every day God is letting you practice and sharpen your people skills with your siblings. I pray that I improve every day. This should be your prayer too. Pray this prayer this week:

*Dear God, please help me to see each of my siblings as the unique and perfect individuals you created them to be. Teach me to celebrate each one and to love them for who they are, not who I want them to be. Give me patience and forgive me for the times I haven't been that way. In Jesus' name, Amen.*

Ready, Set, Grow!

This week I want to work harder at celebrating my siblings' differences by

. . . . . . . . . . . . . . . . . . . . . . . . . . . . . . . . . . . . . . . . . . . . . . . . . . . .

. . . . . . . . . . . . . . . . . . . . . . . . . . . . . . . . . . . . . . . . . . . . . . . . . . . .

. . . . . . . . . . . . . . . . . . . . . . . . . . . . . . . . . . . . . . . . . . . . . . . . . . . .

. . . . . . . . . . . . . . . . . . . . . . . . . . . . . . . . . . . . . . . . . . . . . . . . . . . .

Speak Life

"STICKS AND STONE may break my bones, but words can never harm me." These are words in an old children's rhyme dating back to the early 1800s. It was to give kids a response when bullies taunted them. A few years ago, I was honored to work with an anti-bullying campaign and I became more aware of how powerful our words can be. In spite of what this children's verse tries to say and do, words do hurt people.

Words are mighty. A simple comment has the power to destroy a person or change their life for good. I love to read all the encouraging comments on my social media account, but every day someone will put up something that is not encouraging. In fact, every day I could read hundreds of ugly comments about me and my family. I choose not to read them. For those of you not in the public eye, it's the same. Every day someone can say something to you that can harm you. The fact that this children's rhyme was written in the 1800s tells me bullying is not new. Think about our friend David who killed the giant. The giant teased and bullied David, but David had the last word with a single stone. Now don't get your slingshot out! There are better ways to fight bullies.

If you will think of your words like toothpaste in a tube, it will help you keep your words kind and considerate. Once a word is squeezed out, like toothpaste, you can't put it back in, especially now with social media. One thing that a keyboard has that we don't have is a delete button. We do have the power to write and rewrite something before it is posted on-line. But in our talking life, there's no way to get a word back or delete it once it's been said. Only by realizing the power of our words can we control what we say.

Your words can build up or destroy, encourage or criticize, make someone laugh or cry. The Bible tells us in the book of James to "tame" our tongue. To tame seems like an unusual way to talk about our tongues, but God knows the power of our words, and He also knows our tongues can get away from us like a wild horse.

## What Does the Bible Say about It?

**Proverbs 15:4 (NIV)**
*The soothing tongue is a tree of life, but a perverse tongue crushes the spirit.*

It was difficult to come up with one verse to define this week's study because the Bible is full of "tongue" verses. Obviously God is concerned with this subject and we need to pay attention. I love this verse in Proverbs 15:4. It really captures the message that with our tongues we have the power to either speak life into someone or to crush them.

The Bible uses several descriptive words to describe the destructive power of the tongue. See if you can find them in the following verses.

**Proverbs 12:18:** *Pierce like a* . . . . . . . . . . . . . . . . . . . . . . . . . . .

**Psalm 21:6:** *Like a fleeting* . . . . . . . . . . . . . . . . . . *and a deadly*

. . . . . . . . . . . . . . . . . . . . . . . . .

**Psalm 52:2:** *Like a sharpened* . . . . . . . . . . . . . . . . . . . . . . . . . . . . . . .

The Bible also tells us of the positive power of our tongue.

**Proverbs 21:23:** *Keeps you from* . . . . . . . . . . . . . . . . . . . . . . . . . . . . .

**Proverbs 12:18:** *Brings* . . . . . . . . . . . . . . . . . . . . . . . . . . . . . . . . . . . .

**Psalm 119:172:** *Sing* . . . . . . . . . . . . . . . . . . . . . . . . . . . . . . . . . . . . . .

Controlling our tongues can be challenging. We all think what we have to say is more important than what others have to say. But being silent can bring blessings. I don't mean to always be silent—that would be silly. I just mean stop and think before you speak. If we stop and think first, we might not talk so much. My great-grandma says, "If you can't say anything nice, don't say anything at all." That's a pretty good principle to live by.

Another scripture I love about the tongue is James 1:26: "Those who consider themselves religious and yet do not keep a tight rein on their tongues deceive themselves, and their religion is worthless." Wow! These are pretty strong words. If you claim to be a Christian but use your words to hurt others, your claim of being a Christian will not stand up. Use some self-evaluation time. Have you been guilty of spreading gossip? Have you hurt someone's feelings to build yourself up? Have you yelled at your parents or siblings? Have you said things you regret? If you said yes to any of those questions, it's time to stop. It's time to give your words over to God. Pray God will help you rein in your tongue and instead use it to speak life.

## ❧ Ready, Set, Grow! ❧

This week I will control my tongue when

. . . . . . . . . . . . . . . . . . . . . . . . . . . . . . . . . . . . . . . . . . . . . . . . . . . . . .

. . . . . . . . . . . . . . . . . . . . . . . . . . . . . . . . . . . . . . . . . . . . . . . . . . . . . .

. . . . . . . . . . . . . . . . . . . . . . . . . . . . . . . . . . . . . . . . . . . . . . . . . . . . . .

## Talk About It

ONE OF THE THINGS I am most grateful about in my family is we talk about everything—and I mean everything! Once you've talked about STDs with your grandpa, there's nothing left to hide. You might come from a family that's not as open as mine, but I challenge you to encourage your family to find a way to talk.

At my Two-Mama's house, she keeps a box of "table talk" discussion cards on her kitchen table. All the grandkids love to be the one to read the questions during mealtime. Of course these conversations aren't quite as embarrassing as a talk about STDs, but it's a way to get the family talking and a way to find out what your grandparents did on their first date.

So, why don't families talk more? I guess every family is different and has their reasons, but I think there are a few reasons we all have in common. One, I'm probably as guilty as you are about looking down at my phone when I shouldn't. Seriously, we've got to put our phones down and start looking at and talking to the people we love the most. Two, many of us have our own rooms where we can hide out from our family members. And the third reason might be we're afraid to open up to our parents about things going on in our lives.

That last one is the one I want to focus on. We all need someone to talk to, and best friends are great, and I love to talk to my friends, but they are usually the same age as me. Their experiences aren't very different from mine, so advice from them is limited. Your parents have lived life longer, love you the most, and have your best interests at heart. I know, not all parents are great parents and I can't change that, but most of our parents love us and want the best for us. They just need us to talk to them. Have you ever heard the expression "You don't know what you don't know"? You may have to read that again. But basically, your parents can't help you if you never tell them what's going on. So, it's simple. Just talk. If you don't have a parent to talk to, reach out to a teacher, youth leader, grandparent, or other relative. I promise, reaching out to someone will bless them as much as it will help you.

## What Does the Bible Say about It?

**2 John 1:12 (NIV)**
*I have much to write to you, but I do not want to use paper and ink. Instead, I hope to visit you and talk with you face to face, so that our joy may be complete.*

This book of 2 John in the Bible deals with more issues than our simple lesson on the importance of talking. Let's break down the verse and see what we can learn from it. Under each line, write the verse in your own words.

*I have much to write to you*

. . . . . . . . . . . . . . . . . . . . . . . . . . . . . . . . . . . . . . . . . . . . . . . . . . . . . . . . . . . . . . . . . . . .

. . . . . . . . . . . . . . . . . . . . . . . . . . . . . . . . . . . . . . . . . . . . . . . . . . . . . . . . . . . . . . . . . . . .

. . . . . . . . . . . . . . . . . . . . . . . . . . . . . . . . . . . . . . . . . . . . . . . . . . . . . . . . . . . . . . . . . . . .

*But I do not want to use paper and ink.*

. . . . . . . . . . . . . . . . . . . . . . . . . . . . . . . . . . . . . . . . . . . . . . . . . . . . . . . . . . . . . . . . . . . .

. . . . . . . . . . . . . . . . . . . . . . . . . . . . . . . . . . . . . . . . . . . . . . . . . . . . . . . . . . . . . . . . . . . .

. . . . . . . . . . . . . . . . . . . . . . . . . . . . . . . . . . . . . . . . . . . . . . . . . . . . . . . . . . . . . . . . . . . .

*Instead, I hope to visit you and talk with you face to face*

. . . . . . . . . . . . . . . . . . . . . . . . . . . . . . . . . . . . . . . . . . . . . . . . . . . . . . . . . . . . . . . . . . . .

. . . . . . . . . . . . . . . . . . . . . . . . . . . . . . . . . . . . . . . . . . . . . . . . . . . . . . . . . . . . . . . . . . . .

. . . . . . . . . . . . . . . . . . . . . . . . . . . . . . . . . . . . . . . . . . . . . . . . . . . . . . . . . . . . . . . . . . . .

*So that our joy may be complete.*

. . . . . . . . . . . . . . . . . . . . . . . . . . . . . . . . . . . . . . . . . . . . . . . . . . . . . . . . . . . . . . . . . . . .

. . . . . . . . . . . . . . . . . . . . . . . . . . . . . . . . . . . . . . . . . . . . . . . . . . . . . . . . . . . . . . . . . . . .

. . . . . . . . . . . . . . . . . . . . . . . . . . . . . . . . . . . . . . . . . . . . . . . . . . . . . . . . . . . . . . . . . . . .

In the verse we can feel the importance of talking face-to-face. In today's terms, the verse might say, "I have tons to tell you, but I don't want to text it. I want to tell you in person so I can see the expression on your face." There are more than a few negatives about our new texting world, but one thing I have found very difficult is knowing what someone is feeling in a text. The emoticons definitely help, but still, it's hard to know exactly how someone feels about a certain thing until you talk to them—face-to-face. I truly love this verse and the message it sends. If you want to have a closer relationship with your parents, talk to them. If you want to get along better with your siblings, talk to them. You might want to have a box of table talk cards. Take one night or a Sunday afternoon and have everyone in the family write five questions they would like to talk about on five different note cards. These can be as simple as "If you could go anywhere, where would you go?" or more difficult, like "Who is your hero in the faith? And why?" The questions aren't as important as the answers. So, ask away and enjoy!

## Ready, Set, Grow!

This week I will take steps to talk to my family more by

. . . . . . . . . . . . . . . . . . . . . . . . . . . . . . . . . . . . . . . . . .

. . . . . . . . . . . . . . . . . . . . . . . . . . . . . . . . . . . . . . . . . .

. . . . . . . . . . . . . . . . . . . . . . . . . . . . . . . . . . . . . . . . . .

## Temples to Protect

WHEN I WAS THIRTEEN, I got to travel to Austria to play basketball for the Junior Olympics. It was an awesome experience and I learned so much, on and off the court. Well, you can't go to Austria without visiting a castle or two. They are so amazing! Standing in front of a castle that dates back to the eleventh or twelfth century is crazy and makes you realize that America is really, really young.

One of the castles I loved is named Burg Hohenwerfen (so happy I don't have to pronounce that). All castles have one thing in common: they are built to protect something or someone. They are usually built on a mountain that is difficult to get to, and they are often surrounded by an extremely high wall with all kinds of things built to deter an attack. There might be a moat and several guards strategically placed to further ensure safety. This particular castle, Hohenwerfen, was attacked in the early 1500s and was nearly burned to the ground. It's sad to think of someone deliberately destroying something so beautiful.

Keep that image in your brain as you read 1 Corinthians 6:19–20 (NIV) with me.

*Do you not know that your bodies are temples of the Holy Spirit, who is in you, whom you have received from God? You are not your own; you were bought at a price. Therefore honor God with your bodies.*

A castle isn't exactly a temple, but you get the point. If a castle, no matter how elaborate, is torn down, it can be rebuilt. After Hohenwerfen was nearly burned to the ground, it was rebuilt in the 1560s and has gone on to live a long and productive castle life. But our human, fleshly body cannot be rebuilt if it's destroyed. We are given one chance at taking care of what God gave us. Please, know this, God can rebuild the life of anyone who has messed up or made mistakes, but sometimes healing can take a while. The best thing to do is to protect your heart, mind, and soul. Once I heard someone say it's easier to prevent a disease than to cure it. That makes sense to me.

You may not like everything about your body. I don't. But it's yours and the one you've been given. So instead of comparing your body to others, be grateful for it—there's always someone out there who has it worse.

Remember we were paid for with a high price tag—the death of Jesus Christ. Your job is to honor your body and take care of it. In doing this, you will honor God.

**Mark 12:30 (NIV)**
*Love the Lord your God with all your heart and with all your soul and with all your mind and with all your strength.*

—❦❦❦— Dig a Little Deeper —❦❦❦—

Just like a castle is built out of several different materials, we are too. To protect a castle, the king had to put into place those things that would guard against attackers. We must do the same. Read Mark 12:30 and fill in the blanks.

*Love the Lord your God with all your . . . . . . . . . . . . . and with all your . . . . . . . . . . . . . and with all your . . . . . . . . . . . . . and with all your . . . . . . . . . . . . . .*

From this verse we see the four areas that make us who we are: heart, soul, mind, and body. Another way to say it would be emotional, spiritual, mental, and physical.

Mark 12:30 also gives us one way to protect the temple God has put us in. What is that way?

. . . . . . . . . . . . . . . . . . . . . . . . . . . . . . . . . . . . . . . . . . . . . . . . . . . . . . . .
. . . . . . . . . . . . . . . . . . . . . . . . . . . . . . . . . . . . . . . . . . . . . . . . . . . . . . . .
. . . . . . . . . . . . . . . . . . . . . . . . . . . . . . . . . . . . . . . . . . . . . . . . . . . . . . . .
. . . . . . . . . . . . . . . . . . . . . . . . . . . . . . . . . . . . . . . . . . . . . . . . . . . . . . . .

Yes, it simply says to love the Lord in each of these areas. How would you show God you love Him with your physical body?

. . . . . . . . . . . . . . . . . . . . . . . . . . . . . . . . . . . . . . . . . . . . . . . . . . . . .

. . . . . . . . . . . . . . . . . . . . . . . . . . . . . . . . . . . . . . . . . . . . . . . . . . . . .

. . . . . . . . . . . . . . . . . . . . . . . . . . . . . . . . . . . . . . . . . . . . . . . . . . . . .

Emotional?

. . . . . . . . . . . . . . . . . . . . . . . . . . . . . . . . . . . . . . . . . . . . . . . . . . . . .

. . . . . . . . . . . . . . . . . . . . . . . . . . . . . . . . . . . . . . . . . . . . . . . . . . . . .

. . . . . . . . . . . . . . . . . . . . . . . . . . . . . . . . . . . . . . . . . . . . . . . . . . . . .

Spiritual?

. . . . . . . . . . . . . . . . . . . . . . . . . . . . . . . . . . . . . . . . . . . . . . . . . . . . .

. . . . . . . . . . . . . . . . . . . . . . . . . . . . . . . . . . . . . . . . . . . . . . . . . . . . .

. . . . . . . . . . . . . . . . . . . . . . . . . . . . . . . . . . . . . . . . . . . . . . . . . . . . .

Mental?

. . . . . . . . . . . . . . . . . . . . . . . . . . . . . . . . . . . . . . . . . . . . . . . . . . . . .

. . . . . . . . . . . . . . . . . . . . . . . . . . . . . . . . . . . . . . . . . . . . . . . . . . . . .

. . . . . . . . . . . . . . . . . . . . . . . . . . . . . . . . . . . . . . . . . . . . . . . . . . . . .

## Live It!

Loving God means honoring and obeying Him. Remember, God never gives us a rule or boundary just to be mean. He always does it to protect us. He knows what is best for us. We don't. We're human and can only see what our human eyes can see. God's vision takes us all the way to Heaven. If we want to protect our mental health, we have to fill our minds with things that challenge us and help us grow. To protect our emotional health, we don't act from just our feelings but instead know God's unchanging Word and plan for us. If we want to protect our spiritual health, we have to spend time with God, read God's Word, and fill our minds with words of wisdom from the Bible. If we want to protect our physical health, we have to exercise, eat healthy foods, and treat our bodies respectfully. It's all about choices. Choose those things that help your "temple" stay strong.

## Ready, Set, Grow!

This week I will work to protect my temple by

. . . . . . . . . . . . . . . . . . . . . . . . . . . . . . . . . . . . . . . . . . . . . . . . . . . . . . .

. . . . . . . . . . . . . . . . . . . . . . . . . . . . . . . . . . . . . . . . . . . . . . . . . . . . . . .

. . . . . . . . . . . . . . . . . . . . . . . . . . . . . . . . . . . . . . . . . . . . . . . . . . . . . . .

. . . . . . . . . . . . . . . . . . . . . . . . . . . . . . . . . . . . . . . . . . . . . . . . . . . . . . .

## *Under the Blood*

MOST CHURCHGOING PEOPLE are familiar with the song "Amazing Grace." My great-grandpa was a song leader, and I can still remember him up in front of the church, leading songs like "Amazing Grace" and "Victory in Jesus." My home church has a large Celebrate Recovery ministry, so this song is almost a battle cry for the men and women who have been involved in some type of addiction and have been set free by the blood of Jesus.

The blood of Jesus isn't reserved only for those who have been addicted to drugs or lost in pornography or caught up in anger issues. The blood of Jesus is for everyone. I've heard people jokingly say, "He's working on his testimony," meaning he's living in sin a while and then he'll come back to the Lord. It just doesn't work like that. Either you're with God or you're not. Being a child of God doesn't mean you're perfect and sin-free. No one is perfect except Jesus. Being a child of God means you know where your salvation comes from and you have declared that Jesus is the Lord of your life.

Acts 2:38 tells us that repentance leads us to be baptized. Baptism is symbolic of the death, burial, and resurrection of Jesus. Jesus shed His blood for everyone. When we are dipped under the water in baptism, we are doing more than getting clean from the day's dirt. We are being cleaned and set free from all our sins. There isn't one person—from the worst sinner to the newest baby—who Jesus' blood won't cover.

Yes, it's God's amazing grace that saves each one of us. Without it, we would be lost.

## What Does the Bible Say about It?

**1 John 1:7 (NIV)**
*But if we walk in the light, as he is in the light, we have fellowship with one another, and the blood of Jesus, his Son, purifies us from all sin.*

## Dig a Little Deeper

This whole first chapter of 1 John is as exciting to read today as it must have been when it was first written. This letter doesn't tell us who wrote it or who it was written to, though most scholars think the author was the apostle John. Whoever wrote it loved the people he wrote to, and he was passionate about what he was sharing. We also know that the words apply to all believers. List five reasons why this letter, 1 John, was written.

1. 1 John 1:3: *To verify that we have fellowship with the* . . . . . . . . . . . . . . . . . . . . . . . . . . . . . . . *and* . . . . . . . . . . . . . . . . . .

2. 1 John 1:4: *To make our joy* . . . . . . . . . . . . . . . . . . . . . .

3. 1 John 2:1: *So you will not* . . . . . . . . . . . . . . . . . . . . . . .

4. 1 John 2:26: *I am writing these things to you about those who are trying to lead you* . . . . . . . . . . . . . . . . . . . . . . . . . . .

5. 1 John 5:13: *So you may know that you have* . . . . . . . . . . . . .

I'm sure the early church members were excited to read these words. The letter was probably written because they had been struggling with these things. It would be like one of us speaking to our youth group about something they had been dealing with. It's important to remember the early church dealt with the same problems we deal with today. 1 John 2:19 tells us that some of the church members had stopped believing and had gone out causing trouble. That still happens today, doesn't it? Friends who were once strong believers begin to act ungodly and try to take others with them. 1 John warns against this. Fill in the blanks in these powerful few verses in 1 John 1:5–7 (NIV).

*This is the message we have heard from him and declare to you: God is* . . . . . . . . . . . . . . . . . *; in him there is no* . . . . . . . . . . . . . . *at all. If we claim to have* . . . . . . . . . . . . . . . . . *with him and yet*

*walk in the* ........................., *we lie and do not live out the*
.......................... *But if we walk in the* ......................., *as he is in*
*the light, we have* ......................... *with one another, and the*
.......................................... *of Jesus, his Son, purifies us from*
*all* .................

## Live It!

Knowing and doing are two different things. As we grow in Christ, hopefully our "doing" surpasses our "knowing." I once heard a preacher say, "We don't do what's right so we'll go to Heaven. We do what's right because we're already going there." I love that.

Our decisions to do what is right should be because God has freely given us the gift of eternal life. It's our gratitude to Him that should keep us walking in the light just as he walks in the light. I hope that makes sense. If you are struggling to make right choices, try waking up every morning and saying, first thing, "Thank you, God! I'm going to Heaven!" Repeat those words at least ten times before you brush your teeth or put on your makeup. This way you are sending yourself an important message: Jesus Christ died for you, God loves you, and you will spend eternity with Him.

## Ready, Set, Grow!

This week I will remind myself that it's the blood of Jesus that gives me hope. I will show my thanks to God by

. . . . . . . . . . . . . . . . . . . . . . . . . . . . . . . . . . . . . . . . . . . . . . . . . . .

. . . . . . . . . . . . . . . . . . . . . . . . . . . . . . . . . . . . . . . . . . . . . . . . . . .

. . . . . . . . . . . . . . . . . . . . . . . . . . . . . . . . . . . . . . . . . . . . . . . . . . .

. . . . . . . . . . . . . . . . . . . . . . . . . . . . . . . . . . . . . . . . . . . . . . . . . . .

*Walk Away*

IN MY BOOK *Live Original*, I tell about a time when a "friend" came up and said she needed to tell me something that someone had said about me. I asked her if it would hurt my feelings, and she said yes, but that I needed to hear it. I simply said, "No, I don't," and I walked away.

Walking away is hard to do, isn't it? First of all, we're curious people and we just want to know stuff. Second, we might want to take some kind of action. For me, in that situation, I looked at it more like self-preservation. I knew it wouldn't be good for me to hear something negative about myself. I knew it might make me change who I am and what I'm trying to accomplish in life. I knew it would cause me to focus on myself more, and that's never good. So, I walked away.

The problem with staying and listening or reading negative comments online is we can't just hear negative comments and move on. Usually some action has to take place, and those actions aren't typically healthy. We might start questioning everything about ourselves. *Am I skinny enough? Am I smart enough? Can I really sing well enough for choir? Do I have what it takes to be a cheerleader?* Anytime we allow negative comments to dominate our "self-conversation," we're in danger of heading toward a bad place. While there's always room for growing and being a better person, this kind of a situation allows someone else to influence who you should be.

There's usually a reason people do what they do and say what they say. However, you can't know every reason. You'll go crazy trying to figure it out. Most of the time, my advice is just to walk away. Tell yourself something is going on in that person's life to cause them to hurt others. Life is not easy for any of us. It's a fast-moving roller coaster with lots of twists and turns. During our teen years, sometimes our actions are just not Christ-like and we lash out at others without cause. Every teen you know will one day be an adult with regrets about things they said and did. The only future adult you can control is yourself, and sometimes that means walking away.

## What Does the Bible Say about It?

**Matthew 7:12 (NIV)**
*So in everything, do to others what you would have them do to you, for this sums up the Law and the Prophets.*

 Dig a Little Deeper

Have you heard of the Golden Rule? It says, "Do unto others as you want them to do unto you." This life rule comes from this verse. Matthew 7:12 is part of what is called the Sermon on the Mount.

Read Matthew 5:1–2. Can you figure out why this section of the Bible is called the Sermon on the Mount?

. . . . . . . . . . . . . . . . . . . . . . . . . . . . . . . . . . . . . . . . . . . . . . . . . . . . . . . . . . . . . . . . . . . .

. . . . . . . . . . . . . . . . . . . . . . . . . . . . . . . . . . . . . . . . . . . . . . . . . . . . . . . . . . . . . . . . . . . .

. . . . . . . . . . . . . . . . . . . . . . . . . . . . . . . . . . . . . . . . . . . . . . . . . . . . . . . . . . . . . . . . . . . .

. . . . . . . . . . . . . . . . . . . . . . . . . . . . . . . . . . . . . . . . . . . . . . . . . . . . . . . . . . . . . . . . . . . .

The Golden Rule is very important because, in that one sentence, Jesus defines our Christian behavior. It would have been easy for Jesus to list a bunch of dos and don'ts, but He simply gave us one important do. Jesus knows us, and He knows that we are innately selfish. In fact, look at Matthew 7:11. Jesus calls people . . . . . . . . . . . . . . . . . . . . . . . . . . . . . . . The reason we talk badly about others is we are all selfish on the inside. But we also all want the same things. We want to be shown love, respect, and appreciation. Jesus knew if we would just treat others like we *want* to be treated—loved, respected, appreciated—then the world would be a better place.

The Sermon on the Mount ends in a powerful way. First Jesus says these words in Matthew 7:24:

*Therefore everyone who hears these words of mine and puts them into practice is like a wise man who built his house on the rock.*

This example was something every listener could understand. Jesus went on to describe the foolish man who didn't follow what Jesus said. He was as foolish as a man who would build a house on the sand. I can just imagine the crowd nodding their heads as they understood this principle.

I love how the Sermon on the Mount ends. Read these important words found in Matthew 7:28–29 (NIV):

*When Jesus had finished saying these things, the crowds were amazed at his teaching, because he taught as one who had authority, and not as their teachers of the law.*

The crowd knew Jesus was someone of more importance than the other teachers they had been listening to. When it comes to listening to Jesus, never walk away. Words that come from Him are always worth listening to.

## Live It!

Is there someone in your life you should walk away from? Is someone keeping you from being who you know God wants you to be? Is there someone who tears you down instead of lifting you up? Perhaps you have been friends with someone for a long time, but they have suddenly started being mean to you. It's always best to look at yourself first to see if you are doing anything that would hurt someone else. In another part of the Sermon on the Mount, in Matthew 7:3–5, we're told to not worry about the "speck" in our friend's eye if we have a "plank" in ours. I know that sounds funny, but it's great that Jesus uses examples we can understand. (He's good like that.) We can certainly understand we've got to get the junk out of our own lives before we can complain about someone else. Search yourself honestly to be sure you haven't done anything to offend this person. If you have, go to them and set it straight.

If you haven't done anything wrong, then pray about the person you are struggling with. I've found when I pray about someone, my heart softens toward them and I can understand them better. This doesn't mean that I won't walk away if needed; it just means I don't hold any bitter feelings toward them.

## ❧ Ready, Set, Grow! ❧

This week I will work hard to apply the Golden Rule to all my relationships by

. . . . . . . . . . . . . . . . . . . . . . . . . . . . . . . . . . . . . . . . . . . . . . . . . . . . . . . .

. . . . . . . . . . . . . . . . . . . . . . . . . . . . . . . . . . . . . . . . . . . . . . . . . . . . . . . .

. . . . . . . . . . . . . . . . . . . . . . . . . . . . . . . . . . . . . . . . . . . . . . . . . . . . . . . .

. . . . . . . . . . . . . . . . . . . . . . . . . . . . . . . . . . . . . . . . . . . . . . . . . . . . . . . .

## Who Told You That?

HAVE YOUR PARENTS ever said to you, "Who told you that?" Mine have. Many times I have reported something I heard at school or on Facebook to my mom or dad, and they are quick to say, "Who told you that?"

I've come to realize those are four very powerful words. *Where* we get our information says everything about the value of the information we are getting. We don't have to read very far into the Bible before these four words are said by God.

From the book of Genesis we know God created man and woman. He named them Adam and Eve and gave them the most beautiful place to live—a garden with all the food they could ever want. But God was very clear about one thing: they were not to eat of the Tree of Knowledge of Good and Evil. It doesn't take long for Satan to appear, and in Genesis 3, he uses his sneaky ways by speaking through the form of a serpent to Eve. The serpent (Satan) uses tricky words to confuse Eve and cause her to question God's command. Satan says, "Did God really say . . . ?" Oh, how Satan knows us! All he had to do was place a little doubt in Eve's mind and, sure enough, she would follow him. In Genesis 3 we learn that Eve did eat the fruit and offered it to Adam, and he ate too.

Next the Bible says God was out walking in the garden and Adam and Eve hid from Him because they were naked. God called for them because you really can't hide from God. When they confessed they had hidden because they were naked, God said those powerful words, "Who told you that you were naked?" You see, had they never listened to Satan, had they never taken that bite, had they never doubted God, they would not have known they were naked. They still would have been naked; they just wouldn't have known it. That knowledge wouldn't have affected them.

Who are you listening to? Are you listening to the voices of parents who know and love you? Are you listening to friends you can trust to give you sound advice? Or are you listening to voices that tell you it's okay to have a drink or two on Friday night, or to have sex with a boyfriend because you love him, or it doesn't matter if you cheat at school every now and then? God is asking you the same question he asked Adam and Eve: "Who told you that?" Who tells you sin is okay? The only answer to that question is Satan. From the beginning of time, Satan has used his limited powers to convince humans that God doesn't really want the best for us. Let me tell you this: the only good answer to "Who told you that?" is "God told me that." If you can answer that every time, you will always be on the right track.

**Job 38:2 (NIV)**
*Who is this that obscures my plans with words without knowledge?*

———— Dig a Little Deeper ————

The account of Adam and Eve is very interesting and easy to read. You might want to read through it this week. Remember, every time you read from the Bible you will see something new. Our verse for today is not usually chosen for a devotional, but I really like it. It's found in the book of Job. The book of Job is about a man named Job (makes sense, right?) who really loved God. In fact, he loved God so much that Satan (yes, that tricky guy is always around) tells God he could cause Job to fall away from God. So God agrees to let Satan test Job's faithfulness. After many curses, including the deaths of his family members, Job remained faithful to God. Job's friends and some family members speak up and tell Job that God has deserted him and he should denounce God. Then it's God's time to speak. That is what is found in Job 38 and why I chose this verse to go with this lesson. God basically says the same thing to Job that He said to Adam and Eve: "Who told you that?" What He really says is found in verse 2: "Who is this that obscures my plans with words without knowledge?"

The rest of this chapter is a series of questions. Let's look at a few of them.

Read the following verses and fill in the blanks.

**Job 38:4**
*Where were you when I laid the earth's* ..........................?

**Job 38:8**
*Who shut up the* .......................... *behind doors . . . ?*

**Job 38:35**
*Do you send the* .......................... *bolts on their way? Do they report to* .........................., *'Here we are'?*

This entire chapter is God telling Job and his friends that He is God and they are not. It's also a reminder to us. God is God, and if we listen to anyone else, we are listening to the wrong person. God made it very clear to Job that he was listening to the wrong people. Once Job stopped whining, he was able to hear God's voice.

Read Job 42:2 (NIV) and fill in the blanks.

*I know that you can do* .......................... *things; no purpose of yours can be* ...........................

Who we listen to can either make or break us. Never doubt Satan is alive and active. He knows your strengths and your weaknesses, and he will attack when you least expect it.

What is a strong area for you?

. . . . . . . . . . . . . . . . . . . . . . . . . . . . . . . . . . . . . . . . . . . . . . . . . . . . . .

. . . . . . . . . . . . . . . . . . . . . . . . . . . . . . . . . . . . . . . . . . . . . . . . . . . . . .

. . . . . . . . . . . . . . . . . . . . . . . . . . . . . . . . . . . . . . . . . . . . . . . . . . . . . .

. . . . . . . . . . . . . . . . . . . . . . . . . . . . . . . . . . . . . . . . . . . . . . . . . . . . . .

What is an area of weakness?

. . . . . . . . . . . . . . . . . . . . . . . . . . . . . . . . . . . . . . . . . . . . . . . . . . . . . .

. . . . . . . . . . . . . . . . . . . . . . . . . . . . . . . . . . . . . . . . . . . . . . . . . . . . . .

. . . . . . . . . . . . . . . . . . . . . . . . . . . . . . . . . . . . . . . . . . . . . . . . . . . . . .

. . . . . . . . . . . . . . . . . . . . . . . . . . . . . . . . . . . . . . . . . . . . . . . . . . . . . .

No matter how weak you feel in an area, know that God is stronger. When you begin to doubt God's power, read Job 38 and be reminded. YOUR God is the God who holds back the seas and tells the lightning when to strike. He knows when every mountain goat gives birth, and He gives horses their strength. I'm pretty sure He's capable of getting you or me out of any tough situation we might get in, if only we will listen to Him.

### Ready, Set, Grow!

This week I will not listen to Satan, but will hear the voice of God when

.......................................................................
.......................................................................
.......................................................................
.......................................................................

## Worry No More (I'm Working on It!)

OKAY, YOU CAN TELL by the title this week that I'm a bit of a worrier. In an earlier chapter, I gave a brief description of John Luke and myself (how he loves flying, and I can't wait to land) as a way of letting you know the truth about me: I'm a worrier! There. I said it. Now I can be on the road to recovery, right? The first step to recovering is admitting the problem.

The problem is I've always been a worrier. I do believe you're either born with the worry gene or you're not. I stand in awe of my family members, like John Luke and my mom, who don't seem to have a care in the world. I know they do. They just handle their cares without worrying about them.

My mom is always calm in stressful situations. She really helps me deal with my worry issues because she is so calm. And John Luke got my mom's worry-free gene. At the beach, John Luke gets his scuba license, while I sit on the sand afraid of sharks. I keep an inhaler, though I don't have asthma or allergies. John Luke has both conditions, but he doesn't carry an inhaler. When home alone, I plan my escape route in case something happens. John never thinks anything will happen.

As you can see, worrying is a pastime I participate in, but I don't want to!

I really am trying to work on this. The Bible is full of verses that tell people to not be anxious or worried or afraid, so living a stress-free life must be important to God. I have also learned worry takes away my joy. I don't mean it takes away the deep-down joy I have all the time because I am a daughter of the King, but it can take away the joy or happiness of the moment. When I spend my time worrying a shark will attack me, obviously I'm not enjoying the beauty of the ocean.

Life will always bring its share of things we could worry about, but Jesus puts it in the best way. He says, "Can all your worries add a single moment to your life?" In other words, does worry help? The answer is always no. My Two-Mama, who claims to be a recovering worrier, says worry is like a rocking chair. There's a lot of activity happening, but no one is going anywhere.

## What Does the Bible Say about It?

### Isaiah 41:10 (NIV)
*So do not fear, for I am with you; do not be dismayed, for I am your God. I will strengthen you and help you; I will uphold you with my righteous right hand.*

Isaiah 41:10 is one of my favorite verses in the Bible. My Mamaw Howard went to live with Jesus in 2013, but I still have a recording on my phone of her quoting this verse in the King James Version. Mamaw Howard would always emphasize certain words. Read it aloud and emphasize the words in uppercase below. You will see why this verse was so special to Mamaw and to me.

*So do NOT fear, for I am with you; do NOT be dismayed, for I am your God. I will STRENGTHEN you and HELP you; I will UPHOLD you with MY righteous right hand.*

When my Mamaw Howard quoted that scripture, you could tell she believed it with all her heart, and for good reason. When you read this verse, it's very clear who is in charge of us. God is. He is the one who can conquer all your fears. He is the one to give you boldness when you feel intimidated. He is the one who strengthens you when you feel weak. He is the one who helps you when you feel helpless.

Isaiah was a prophet. Like all prophets, his job was to tell the people of his day about what was to come.

Read Isaiah 7:14. What did Isaiah prophesy?

. . . . . . . . . . . . . . . . . . . . . . . . . . . . . . . . . . . . . . . . . . . . . . . . . . . . . . . . . . . .

. . . . . . . . . . . . . . . . . . . . . . . . . . . . . . . . . . . . . . . . . . . . . . . . . . . . . . . . . . . .

. . . . . . . . . . . . . . . . . . . . . . . . . . . . . . . . . . . . . . . . . . . . . . . . . . . . . . . . . . . .

Isaiah loved God, and he believed what God revealed to him. He spent his lifetime telling others that a Savior would be born. Isaiah 12:2 sums up Isaiah's beliefs. Fill in the blanks to this powerful verse.

*Surely God is my* .......................; *I will trust and not be* .............................. *The* LORD, *the* LORD *himself, is my* ............. *and my* .......................; *he has become my* ...................... .

## Live It!

Living this one out can be a challenge for us "worry warriors." One thing I know is that I can't overcome worrying by myself. I have to totally give my worry to God. This doesn't mean to put your worries in a big sack and throw them out in the yard, only to retrieve them later and carry them around. No, it means to put them in a big sack and throw them away, never to pick them up again. One exercise you can try is to write out the things you're worried about on a piece of paper. Then spend time praying about each one, asking God to do what He feels best in each case. Then, take a match and burn those worries away.

Another thing I have done is replace those worry thoughts with God thoughts. Try memorizing a few short scriptures you can keep in your head to replace a worry thought. Psalm 46:1 is a good one. It says, "God is our refuge and strength, an ever-present help in trouble." When you feel a worry try to sneak in, say this scripture to chase it away.

## ❧ Ready, Set, Grow! ❧

This week I will give my worries to God. I will let Him handle

. . . . . . . . . . . . . . . . . . . . . . . . . . . . . . . . . . . . . . . . . . . . . . . . . . . . . .

. . . . . . . . . . . . . . . . . . . . . . . . . . . . . . . . . . . . . . . . . . . . . . . . . . . . . .

. . . . . . . . . . . . . . . . . . . . . . . . . . . . . . . . . . . . . . . . . . . . . . . . . . . . . .

. . . . . . . . . . . . . . . . . . . . . . . . . . . . . . . . . . . . . . . . . . . . . . . . . . . . . .

## Extra Grace Required

YEARS AGO MY PAPAW PHIL fished to support his family. He had to be very serious about his fishing, and he carefully guarded the river near his home. This was his livelihood. This was how he fed his family.

Some local boys started making trouble one day when they stole some of the fish. They didn't stop with one time. They kept coming back, stealing Papaw's fish. Papaw finally had enough and went outside with a shotgun and yelled that he would shoot them if they did not get off his property—for good! Okay, that would have scared me away for sure! But those boys came back.

It was while all this was going on that Papaw Phil became a Christian. The next time the boys came back, Papaw Phil left his shotgun inside and took his Bible out with him. He told those boys, "Whatever fish you get, you can keep. But you have to come to my house and have a Bible study with me." The boys did just that. They came to the house and studied the Bible and never stole another fish.

Have you ever been in a situation when you retaliated

with a shotgun? Hopefully not. But you probably have used unkind words either in person or on a text or through someone else. Maybe you didn't use any words; maybe you gave a hateful or disgusted look. Any of those responses are sure to make enemies, and enemies will do nothing to advance the kingdom of God.

I realize there are times when someone can be very annoying and do such bad things you want to scream. Those are the people who require extra grace—like the boys who wouldn't stop stealing Papaw's fish. But Papaw learned that hatred and violence don't solve problems; only the good news of Jesus can do that.

## What Does the Bible Say about It?

**James 3:17 (NIV)**
*But the wisdom that comes from heaven is first of all pure; then peace-loving, considerate, submissive, full of mercy and good fruit, impartial and sincere.*

## Dig a Little Deeper

All the way back in weeks six and eleven we looked at the book of James. I love this little book. It's only five chapters, but they are powerful chapters. James is the book to go to if you are wondering how you should act. Its main focus is on how to live practically as a Christian. It's clear James believed Christians show their faith by their actions. Papaw Phil was able to show those fish-stealing guys that a Christian handles situations in a different way. That's exactly what James teaches.

Read James 3:17 and list the wisdoms that come from Heaven or God.

1. ...............................................................................
2. ...............................................................................
3. ...............................................................................
4. ...............................................................................
5. ...............................................................................
6. ...............................................................................
7. ...............................................................................
8. ...............................................................................

Live It!

Treating others with kindness when we are not given kindness in return is hard. It's a discipline to be able to do it. In *Live Original*, I tell the story of a young man who had been diagnosed with cancer and given a short time to live. He didn't die in a short time; he lived for many years. He committed those years to doing good things for others. Sadly, too many of us wait for something bad to happen before we do good things. I would rather think of it like this—something good DID happen, so go out and do good! That something good is that Jesus died for you. That realization is what made my Papaw Phil exchange his shotgun for a Bible (not when hunting, of course). Papaw was so happy that his eternal life would be spared that he wanted to tell others about it. He knew no one would listen to him if he didn't act like he loved God.

Is there someone in your life you have not treated as kindly as you should have? What can you do to fix that situation? Take some time to think about the steps you need to take to show that person who needs extra grace that you love them too and want them to have eternal life.

## ❧ Ready, Set, Grow! ❧

This week I will seek out the person who needs me to show them love by

. . . . . . . . . . . . . . . . . . . . . . . . . . . . . . . . . . . . . . . . . . . . . . . . . . . . . . . . . . . . . . . . . .

. . . . . . . . . . . . . . . . . . . . . . . . . . . . . . . . . . . . . . . . . . . . . . . . . . . . . . . . . . . . . . . . . .

. . . . . . . . . . . . . . . . . . . . . . . . . . . . . . . . . . . . . . . . . . . . . . . . . . . . . . . . . . . . . . . . . .

. . . . . . . . . . . . . . . . . . . . . . . . . . . . . . . . . . . . . . . . . . . . . . . . . . . . . . . . . . . . . . . . . .

## Yes Means Yes

M Y MOM WROTE A BOOK TITLED *Strong and Kind*. It was about character traits my mom and dad feel are important to instill in their children's lives. I'm grateful I have parents who want me to be a good person and work to put good things in my life. I've learned to be strong and kind from many of my family members, but another character trait I've come to value is integrity.

My Papaw Phil started his duck call business back when, as he tells it, "a man's word and a handshake was good enough." In other words, his yes meant yes and his no meant no. I've also learned this important lesson from playing sports. When you commit to play on a sports team in high school, no one asks you to sign a legal agreement (at least, not yet). Most of the time, the decision to play on a high school team is made by hearing an announcement, trying out, and, if you make the team, showing up for the first day of practice. Once you show up the first day, you are committed to the team.

Once I planned to meet my boyfriend on Valentine's Day for an out-of-town date to celebrate. I was playing basketball at the time and an unscheduled game was suddenly announced for the same night. I was so sad! I decided to ask the team what they thought. Should I go with my boyfriend? Should I stay and play? Everyone said I should go except one girl. She said, "You need to stay." And you know what? She was right. I had agreed to play with this team, every game, not just when it was convenient.

Being true to our word isn't about choosing convenience or being comfortable; it's about doing the right thing. As we get older, more and more people will look at us to see if we are people of integrity. Integrity means being honest, truthful, and reliable. One day we'll have a job where our employer will expect us to show up on time and put in a full day's work. We'll have children of our own who will look to us to see how to live a life of integrity. The things you are doing right now are preparing you for the future. Live each day with integrity. Let your yes really mean yes and your no really mean no.

൭ ᷍°໐ඏ What Does the Bible Say about It? ඏ໐°᷍ ൭

**Proverbs 20:11 (NIV)**
*Even small children are known by their actions, so is their conduct really pure and upright?*

Sometimes we tell ourselves we're young so we can act a certain way. This verse in Proverbs tells us that even small children are known for their actions. Think about how true this is. I'm sure you know some small children who are pretty bad kids. Already at a young age, they might lie or cheat or hit or scream or bite. Children who are showing these kinds of behavior are no fun to be around. But this scripture applies to all of us. It's a warning to be sure our conduct is pure and upright. Let's look at a few more scriptures that tell us how God wants us to live.

Read Proverbs 11:1. What does God think about dishonesty?

. . . . . . . . . . . . . . . . . . . . . . . . . . . . . . . . . . . . . . . . . . . . . . . . . . . . .

. . . . . . . . . . . . . . . . . . . . . . . . . . . . . . . . . . . . . . . . . . . . . . . . . . . . .

. . . . . . . . . . . . . . . . . . . . . . . . . . . . . . . . . . . . . . . . . . . . . . . . . . . . .

Read Proverbs 21:3. What is more acceptable to the Lord than sacrifice?

. . . . . . . . . . . . . . . . . . . . . . . . . . . . . . . . . . . . . . . . . . . . . . . . . . . . .

. . . . . . . . . . . . . . . . . . . . . . . . . . . . . . . . . . . . . . . . . . . . . . . . . . . . .

. . . . . . . . . . . . . . . . . . . . . . . . . . . . . . . . . . . . . . . . . . . . . . . . . . . . .

Read Psalm 51:10. What kind of heart should we strive to have?

. . . . . . . . . . . . . . . . . . . . . . . . . . . . . . . . . . . . . . . . . . . . . . . . . . . . .

. . . . . . . . . . . . . . . . . . . . . . . . . . . . . . . . . . . . . . . . . . . . . . . . . . . . .

. . . . . . . . . . . . . . . . . . . . . . . . . . . . . . . . . . . . . . . . . . . . . . . . . . . . .

I told you the story of my basketball game and the decision I made to stay true to my word. Now it's your turn. Write about a time when you had to do the hard thing and stand by your word.

..................................................................

..................................................................

..................................................................

..................................................................

If you haven't experienced a time like this yet, get ready, you will. It might be different from playing in a basketball game instead of going on a date. Maybe you told a friend you would go somewhere, but then you decided the event didn't sound like much fun, so instead of being honest, you told her your mom said you couldn't go. Does that sound more like something that might happen in your life? Whatever it is, people of integrity don't look for excuses. They do what they say they will do and go where they say they will go.

## Ready, Set, Grow!

This week I will show others that I am a person of integrity by

..................................................................

..................................................................

..................................................................

..................................................................

## You Can Only Fix YOU

M Y GRANDMA, the one we call Two-Mama, loves to sew. She has a closet full of little dresses she made for my cousins and me when we were younger. She can't bear to give them away because she made them for us. She even has some she made for my mother (now that's getting pretty old!). It's fun to look at those dresses and realize how much time and energy went into each one. While Two-Mama might be quick to point out the flaws, it would be hurtful if I pointed them out to her.

That's how it is in life too. No one likes to be told they have flaws, yet flaw finding is an activity many of us love to do, and we do it often. My Two-Mama and my mom tell me bullying has always been around, but with social media it is now at a different level. Everyone seems to have an opinion and want to share it. Since *Duck Dynasty* has become popular, our family has seen and heard our share of criticism and hatred. We have also had many messages of love and support. My mom has really helped me put both the criticism and praise in their proper perspective. She says, "Don't believe all the bad things we read *and* don't believe all the good things we read. The truth is always somewhere in the middle." She has a good point.

Even though we're on TV and people think they know us, they really don't. It's just like your friends at school. You know them at school, but you can't know everything that is going on in their lives. When we are quick to judge or find fault in someone, we should stop ourselves with the reminder that we really don't know what is happening to that person. You can only know about you. If you find yourself having a problem with someone at school, don't try to fix them or criticize them. Work on fixing your attitude toward them by getting to know them better and being more compassionate.

## What Does the Bible Say about It?

**Matthew 7:4 (NIV)**
*How can you say to your brother, "Let me take the speck out of your eye," when all the time there is a plank in your own eye?*

## Dig a Little Deeper

During Jesus' time on earth, he walked from city to city, preaching, teaching, and healing the sick.

Matthew 7 is the last chapter in this sermon, and it starts with a warning. Look at verse 1. What is the warning?

Matthew 7:4 asks an important question. Write that question in your own words.

. . . . . . . . . . . . . . . . . . . . . . . . . . . . . . . . . . . . . . . . . . . . . . . . . . . . . . . . .

. . . . . . . . . . . . . . . . . . . . . . . . . . . . . . . . . . . . . . . . . . . . . . . . . . . . . . . . .

. . . . . . . . . . . . . . . . . . . . . . . . . . . . . . . . . . . . . . . . . . . . . . . . . . . . . . . . .

Do you think Jesus knew it would be easier for us to find fault in others than in ourselves?

. . . . . . . . . . . . . . . . . . . . . . . . . . . . . . . . . . . . . . . . . . . . . . . . . . . . . . . . .

. . . . . . . . . . . . . . . . . . . . . . . . . . . . . . . . . . . . . . . . . . . . . . . . . . . . . . . . .

. . . . . . . . . . . . . . . . . . . . . . . . . . . . . . . . . . . . . . . . . . . . . . . . . . . . . . . . .

Why do you think this is true?

. . . . . . . . . . . . . . . . . . . . . . . . . . . . . . . . . . . . . . . . . . . . . . . . . . . . . . . . .

. . . . . . . . . . . . . . . . . . . . . . . . . . . . . . . . . . . . . . . . . . . . . . . . . . . . . . . . .

. . . . . . . . . . . . . . . . . . . . . . . . . . . . . . . . . . . . . . . . . . . . . . . . . . . . . . . . .

### Live It!

Some people misquote these verses in the Bible, saying we shouldn't ever judge the actions of others as being sinful. This verse isn't about whether a person is living in sin or not. This verse was written to remind us that we need to be careful not to reach conclusions about someone without looking closer into their life story. Jesus knew humans have a problem: they like to point a finger at someone else without first looking at their own lives. That was true in Jesus' day and it's true today. Finger-pointing is wrong and has no place among God's people. Does that mean if someone is openly living a sinful life that we turn the other way? No. There are other scriptures that support going to other Christians in love and helping them walk away from sin. But first we should look closely at our own lives and work to get even the appearance of sin out of it before approaching someone about their sin.

We all have things that need to be "fixed." What could you fix about yourself this week?

. . . . . . . . . . . . . . . . . . . . . . . . . . . . . . . . . . . . . . . . . . . . .

. . . . . . . . . . . . . . . . . . . . . . . . . . . . . . . . . . . . . . . . . . . . .

. . . . . . . . . . . . . . . . . . . . . . . . . . . . . . . . . . . . . . . . . . . . .

This would be a good week to apologize to someone you might have misjudged. If you choose to do so, be careful to truly apologize. Telling someone you are sorry they took what you said the wrong way is not an apology. An apology is saying that what you said was wrong.

### Ready, Set, Grow!

This week I will work on me by

. . . . . . . . . . . . . . . . . . . . . . . . . . . . . . . . . . . . . . . . . . . . .

. . . . . . . . . . . . . . . . . . . . . . . . . . . . . . . . . . . . . . . . . . . . .

. . . . . . . . . . . . . . . . . . . . . . . . . . . . . . . . . . . . . . . . . . . . .

## You Can't Hide from You

THERE'S ONE PERSON in the world you can never escape: you can never get away from yourself. One of my dad's friends puts it this way, "Everywhere you go, you're always there." That's why being the best "you" is a great goal.

We've talked some about self-respect, but this week I want us to really focus and understand what that means. The word "respect" means to hold in high regard and admiration. We might respect a certain teacher or our parents or preacher. All of those people are worthy of our respect, and the Bible makes it very clear we should respect them. If you were asked why you respect a certain person you might say things like, "I just love her and admire how she lives her life." Those are the same words you should be able to use about yourself. I'm not talking about in a vain way. I'm talking about in the way God intended it to be.

Respecting ourselves comes when we love ourselves enough to make the right decisions concerning what we do and say and think. God created YOU like no other human being on earth. Even if you have a twin, your twin is not exactly like you.

Do you realize God created you for a unique purpose? He did. "How do I know what my purpose is?" you might ask. I don't know what job you will do or what talent you will use throughout your life, but I do know this: God created us all for one purpose—to love the Lord with all of our hearts and to love others as ourselves.

One of the preachers I admire is Rick Warren. He says in his book *The Purpose Driven Life*, "You were made for God, not vice versa, and life is about letting God use you for his purposes, not you using him for your own purpose."

I love that I don't have to worry (remember, I'm a worrier) about every move I'm going to make. I love that God has a plan for me and He will reveal that plan when it's necessary. But I do want to keep working on being the best I can be so I'm ready when God's plan is revealed. Think about the kind of person you like to spend time with. Are they funny, smart, kind, compassionate, wise, tenderhearted, strong, or convicted? If these are the traits you like to see in others, make sure those are the traits you see in yourself. If you do this, you won't want to hide from yourself—you'll be your own best friend because you'll respect who you are.

## What Does the Bible Say about It?

**Genesis 1:27 (NIV)**
*So God created mankind in his own image, in the image of God he created them; male and female he created them.*

I do not have all the answers to biblical questions, but I do know God wants us to read His Word and He will give us understanding. In Genesis 1:27, I read that God created man. Man didn't evolve from an explosion. God created him (and her). This verse tells us man was created in the image of God. If I make a cake in the image of a cake my Mamaw Kay makes, it won't be the same, but it will have the same qualities. How awesome is it that God gifted you and me with the same qualities He has? We definitely have qualities God didn't give to animals or plants. We have the ability to think, make choices, work, and love others. We can distinguish between right and wrong. We can dream, create, and laugh. We can make good choices, do good things, and we can choose to have good character traits. Read Galatians 5:22–23. These verses describe the fruits of the spirit. These fruits are qualities we all can have. List the nine fruits found in these verses.

1. ...........................................................................

2. ...........................................................................

3. ...........................................................................

4. ...........................................................................

5. ...........................................................................

6. ...........................................................................

7. ...........................................................................

8. ...........................................................................

9. ...........................................................................

In order for *you* to be the kind of person *you* would like to spend time with, *you* must live a life worthy of being your own best friend. Set your life standards high and self-respect will follow you. Don't let others keep you from being the kind of person you want to be. One way to do this is in the area of purity. When girls don't respect themselves enough to keep their bodies pure, a lifetime of regret follows them. Make it your goal to stay pure and make that goal known at the beginning of any relationship. If you are in a dating relationship now and you have not talked about this with your boyfriend—do it today! The Bible says to "flee" from sexual immorality. Synonyms for "flee" are "run," "escape," "fly," and "bolt." Are you getting the picture? God doesn't say, "Just keep kissing. You'll be okay. You can stay strong. It doesn't matter that you're alone in a parked car and no one can see." No, God says run, bolt, fly, FLEE! The best thing is to not put yourself in that kind of situation. Don't be home alone together. Don't be in each other's bedrooms. Pray before, during, and after a date. If all of that doesn't work to keep a boy off of you, my Uncle Jason says to "cull him." I cover this more in my book *Live Original*, but I hope you're getting the picture. You are worth respecting! If you have made some mistakes in the past—no worries. God is a God of second chances. Start now. Change your way of thinking and doing things. You'll be right where God needs you to be, and He will continue with the plans He has for you.

## Ready, Set, Grow!

This week I will work on respecting myself and loving who God made me to be by

. . . . . . . . . . . . . . . . . . . . . . . . . . . . . . . . . . . . . . . . . . . . . . . . . . . . .

. . . . . . . . . . . . . . . . . . . . . . . . . . . . . . . . . . . . . . . . . . . . . . . . . . . . .

. . . . . . . . . . . . . . . . . . . . . . . . . . . . . . . . . . . . . . . . . . . . . . . . . . . . .

. . . . . . . . . . . . . . . . . . . . . . . . . . . . . . . . . . . . . . . . . . . . . . . . . . . . .

## Zap It!

WE LIVE IN THE SOUTH, which means our summer nights are spent swatting things. From mosquitoes to horseflies, bugs are a big part of our summer. We've try everything—mosquito zappers shaped like little tennis rackets, an assortment of insect repellents, citronella candles, bags of sugar water hanging in the garage, repelling wristbands, fly guns—you name it, we've tried it. With the ever-present danger of serious disease, the bottom line is we have to zap anything that threatens to harm us.

I was thinking about this one day as I was zapping a fly that was threatening to eat our watermelon and decided this is how we need to face the devil—with a devil zapper!

One of my mom's friends likes to say the devil is a mouse with a microphone. That is so true. Satan has no power that God hasn't given to him, yet he brags, boasts, and threatens like he is all-powerful. God is the only one who is all-powerful. God knows all, sees all, creates all, controls all, and can confront all. It's with His mighty power that we can be powerful enough to fight off the devil's evil ways.

At camp one summer, our young campers sang a song about this. It was called "Full Armor of God," by NewSpring Church. In it, the lyrics say, "Put on the full armor of God. Stand strong against the evil one." In the closing program of camp, the kids sang the song, then quoted Ephesians 6:11. For the last part of the verse, "Stand against the devil's evil schemes," they would tap their fingers together like they were plotting something. I know this little song, the verse, and those hand symbols will help them to stand against the devil. The armor of God is our devil zapper!

What Does the Bible Say about It?

**Ephesians 6:11 (NIV)**
*Put on the full armor of God, so that you can take your stand against the devil's schemes.*

Dig a Little Deeper

Spiritual warfare is real and happening right now. That's why we are given instructions on how to arm ourselves for the battle. We're told in Ephesians 6:11 to put on our full armor, but what does that mean? Look in Ephesians 6:13–17 (NIV) and fill in the blanks.

*Therefore put on the full armor of . . . . . . . . . . . . . . . , so that when the day of evil comes, you may be able to . . . . . . . . . . . . . . . your ground, and after you have done everything, to stand.*[14] *Stand firm then, with the belt of .............. buckled around your waist, with the .............. of righteousness in place,*[15] *and with your feet fitted with the .............. that comes from the gospel of peace.*[16] *In addition to all this, take up the .............. of faith, with which you can extinguish all the flaming arrows of the evil one.*[17] *Take the .............. of salvation and the .............. of the Spirit, which is the word of God.*

Now list the six ways we can arm ourselves against the devil.

1. ...........................................................
2. ...........................................................
3. ...........................................................
4. ...........................................................
5. ...........................................................
6. ...........................................................

## Live It!

No one would go into battle without the proper equipment. I don't even play basketball without knee pads! Let's equip ourselves for the battle against the devil by filling our heads with Bible verses and songs of praise. I've read so many accounts of near-death experiences. Being close to death is a time when there is nothing left to do but pray. But let's not keep prayer as a last resort. If you don't already start and end your day in prayer, start today.

Praying about your upcoming day tells God you trust Him with it. It lets God know that you know you can't do it alone and you need His constant support.

Praying at the end of the day tells God you can rest in the safety of His hands. Praying is just one way to equip yourself against the devil, but it's a big one. It will change your life!

### ❧ Ready, Set, Grow! ❧

This week I will zap the devil's evil ways by

. . . . . . . . . . . . . . . . . . . . . . . . . . . . . . . . . . . . . . . . . . . . . . . . . . . . . .

. . . . . . . . . . . . . . . . . . . . . . . . . . . . . . . . . . . . . . . . . . . . . . . . . . . . . .

. . . . . . . . . . . . . . . . . . . . . . . . . . . . . . . . . . . . . . . . . . . . . . . . . . . . . .

. . . . . . . . . . . . . . . . . . . . . . . . . . . . . . . . . . . . . . . . . . . . . . . . . . . . . .